ISBN 978-1-5283-3670-3
PIBN 10914479

For support please visit www.forgottenbooks.com

English
Français
Deutsche
Italiano
Español
Português

www.forgottenbooks.com

Mythology Photography **Fiction**
Fishing Christianity **Art** Cooking
Essays Buddhism Freemasonry
Medicine **Biology** Music **Ancient
Egypt** Evolution Carpentry Physics
Dance Geology **Mathematics** Fitness
Shakespeare **Folklore** Yoga Marketing
Confidence Immortality Biographies
Poetry **Psychology** Witchcraft
Electronics Chemistry History **Law**
Accounting **Philosophy** Anthropology
Alchemy Drama Quantum Mechanics
Atheism Sexual Health **Ancient History**
Entrepreneurship Languages Sport
Paleontology Needlework Islam
Metaphysics Investment Archaeology
Parenting Statistics Criminology
Motivational

THE LAW RELATING TO THE BLIND

BY

PHILIP F. SKOTTOWE, LL.B.

Of the Middle Temple, Barrister-at-Law.

WITH A FOREWORD

BY

CAPTAIN IAN FRASER, C.B.E., M.P.

Chairman of St. Dunstan's.

LONDON :

BUTTERWORTH & CO. (PUBLISHERS) LTD.,

BELL YARD, TEMPLE BAR.

SYDNEY :	
MELBOURNE :	BUTTERWORTH & CO. (AUSTRALIA), LTD.
CALCUTTA :	
MADRAS :	BUTTERWORTH & CO. (INDIA), LTD.
BOMBAY :	
TORONTO :	BUTTERWORTH & CO. (CANADA), LTD.
WELLINGTON (N.Z.) :	BUTTERWORTH & CO. (AUSTRALIA), LTD.

1933

HU1942

S copy

PRINTED IN GUERNSEY, C.I., BRITISH ISLES,
BY THE STAR AND GAZETTE COMPANY LTD.

THIS BOOK IS DEDICATED TO

E. T.

FOREWORD.

WHY should there be legislation for the Blind as a special class ? Probably there is no logical answer to this question. Certainly the Blind are much more severely handicapped from an economic point of view than the deaf or the crippled, and this distinguishes them as a class apart from other disabled persons, and justifies special legislation on their behalf. In addition there is a peculiar sentiment for the Blind, and there is a larger number of persons incapacitated by blindness than by any other single disability of the same magnitude. Another point may be that, although definition of any class is difficult, it is easier for practical purposes to define blindness, and to treat those coming within the definition as belonging to a special class than to define other disabilities and classify those who suffer from them. The phrase, " the world of the Blind ", indicates how the popular imagination can appreciate the peculiar position of this class, and can isolate them from the rest of mankind. We seldom hear the phrases " the world of the deaf " or " the world of the crippled ", and such conceptions are difficult.

Perhaps imagination, not reason, is the principal answer to the question. Every seeing person can imagine himself blind ; it is so easy to achieve blindness by merely closing the eyelids, or by trying

vii

to find the way in a really dark place. Moreover, fear of the darkness is instinctive.

Whatever the reason, there are more laws and regulations relating to the Blind than to any other physically handicapped class of citizens.

Not so long ago the great majority of blind people had no option but to secure the means of existence by begging or by selling goods in the street to compassionate passers-by. They were compelled to demonstrate their affliction and to emphasise the fact that they were unfortunate, abnormal creatures.

Nowadays the legislature, following the example of private philanthropy, has provided special educational facilities for the Blind, and has made provision so that practically all blind persons who can contribute by earning towards their maintenance, are given the opportunity to do so, while those who are unemployable are given subsistence allowances. The Statute Book, in special Acts of Parliament for the Blind, and in many clauses of general Acts, bears witness to this change of attitude.

As a result of the provisions made under these enactments, an increasing number of blind persons are able to take pride in regarding themselves, and in seeking to be regarded by others, as normal rather than exceptional individuals.

Nevertheless, the handicap of blindness, however regarded, imposes certain restrictions upon the person suffering it, and obliges him to act in a special manner in connection with certain ordinary transactions in life, such as the making of a contract, or of a will.

Those blind themselves and those who are charged with their well-being, whether in Government or Local Government offices, or in the administration of Charities for the Blind, should know something about the rights and duties of these people under the law.

This book describes the rights and duties of the Blind in a readable and useful manner, and strikes a happy mean between mere readability and dry facts and references, and should be of real interest and use to a very large number of educated blind persons as well as to those who are concerned with their well-being.

Mr. Skottowe tells me that he was urged to write this book by his friendship with a young British blinded soldier who, having been trained and re-educated at St. Dunstan's, pursued a successful professional career. Admiration for his friend, combined with a desire to help those who are engaged in rehabilitation work, is a sufficient reason, and the blind community owes a debt of gratitude to Mr. Skottowe for his interest in their affairs, and his diligence in preparing the book, and to Messrs. Butterworth & Co. for their generosity in publishing it.

IAN FRASER.

PREFACE.

THE Blind population of England and Wales amounted, in 1931, to the very considerable figure of 60,598. Responsibility for their education, training and welfare rests with the Voluntary Agencies and the Local Authorities, and it is with the primary object of providing these Bodies with a comprehensive survey of the law relating to blind persons that this book has been written.

No attempt has before been made to collect and systematically arrange all the cases, statutes, statutory rules and orders, and Departmental memoranda having reference to the legal position of the Blind. The present text-book will therefore, it is hoped, supply a need of legal practitioners and members of the general public who are interested in this subject, as well as of those Agencies and Local Authorities who are directly concerned with the Blind.

The text of the Blind Voters Bill, which was introduced into the House of Commons on February 23, 1933, is included in an Appendix.

The author wishes to express his gratitude to that great organisation of St. Dunstan's, to whose inspiration this volume owes its existence.

P.F.S.

CONTENTS.

xiii

TABLE OF STATUTES.

TABLE OF STATUTES.

TABLE OF CASES.

A.

B.

C.

E.

S.

V.

W.

Law Relating to the Blind.

CHAPTER 1.

THE BLIND AT COMMON LAW

THE recognition of the Blind as a specific subject for legislative enactment is not of modern date. Express reference to blind persons appears in the great Poor Law Act of Elizabeth, 1601, and the reference in the Preamble to 43 Elizabeth, c. 4, to " impotent persons ", may be taken to include the Blind, a suggestion which was made, but left unanswered, by Parker, J., in *Re Elliott* (1910).(*a*)

Contracts.

The Common Law also has taken account of blindness. Blind persons are peculiarly open to deception, fraud upon a blind man being as old as the story of Jacob and Isaac. Accordingly, it was laid down in *Pigot's Case* (1614) (*b*) that, while a blind man may bind himself by deed by having it read over to him, if the deed is misread, it does not bind him, " because

(*a*) 102 L.T. 528.
(*b*) 11 Co. Rep. 28a.

all his understanding in such a case is by his hearing ".(*a*). To the same effect was *Shulter's Case* (1611).(*b*)   The right to avoid such a deed is independent of fraudulent intent in the reader, for the ground of avoidance is not fraud but rather that the mind of the signer did not go with his signature, and that therefore in law he did not sign the contract with which he is charged.   This appears from a dictum of Byles, J., in *Foster* v. *Mackinnon* (1869).(*c*)

He says :

"If a blind man, or a man who cannot read . . .
"has a written contract falsely read over to him,
"the reader misreading to such a degree that the
"written contract is of a nature altogether different
"from the contract pretended to be read from the
"paper which the blind or illiterate man afterwards
"signs; then, at least if there is no negligence, the
"signature so obtained is of no force.   And it is
"invalid not merely on the ground of fraud, where
"fraud exists, but on the ground that the mind of
"the signer did not accompany the signature ; in
"other words, that he never intended to sign, and
"therefore in contemplation of law never did sign,
"the contract to which his name is appended."

It is to be observed that the right of a blind person to avoid a deed or written instrument which he has signed is subject to two limitations.   In the first

---

(*a*) per Thorpe, J., 11 Co. Rep. 28a.
(*b*) 12 Co. Rep. 90.
(*c*) L.R. 4 C.P. 704, at p. 711.

place, if the blind person is guilty of negligence in signing, and in particular if he signs without requiring the document to be read over to him, he will be estopped from afterwards disputing the validity of the contract.   In the second place, it appears that the right to avoid is limited to the case where the misreading is such as to make the entire contract different from that intended to be signed.   The omission or misreading of one clause, however material, may be ground for rectification, but not for avoidance.   This, at least, was the opinion of Warrington, J., who in *Howatson* v. *Webb* (a) says :

> " It seems to be essential that the contract which
> " the signer means to execute should be of a nature
> " entirely different from the contract in dispute.
> " It will not be contended that if, in reading over a
> " contract to a blind person, the reader merely
> " omits or misreads some material clause, the
> " contract is altogether void.   It may be voidable
> " and it may be a subject for rectification, but it
> " is not void."

Blind Guarantor.

In the case of *Vickers* v. *Bell* (b) a guarantee was upheld although the guarantor was blind and deaf, it being shown that he fully understood the contents of the guarantee, which was explained to him by persons who were accustomed to communicate with him by means of his fingers.

(a) [1907] 1 Ch. 537, at p. 544.
(b) (1864) 9 L.T. 600.

Blind Witness of Deed.

Where a deed has been witnessed by a person who has since become blind, it was formerly considered unnecessary to call him as a witness in an action on the deed, proof of his handwriting being regarded as sufficient. In the case of *Pedlar* v. *Paige* (1833) (*a*) proof of handwriting was admitted, following a decision of Holt, C. J., in *Wood* v. *Drury* (1699).(*b*) These cases, however, were not followed in *Cronk* v. *Frith* (1839) (*c*) and *Rees* v. *Williams* (1847),(*d*) and it is now clear that the blind witness must be called, Lord Abinger remarking in *Cronk* v. *Frith* that " he might from his recollection of the transaction give most important evidence respecting it ".(*e*)

Publication of Libel.

There may be publication of a libel to a blind man by reading the defamatory statement to him. In *Morgan* v. *Wallis* (1917) (*f*) it was alleged that a defamatory bill of costs was published to a typist and to the client who was blind and had to have the defamatory words read to him " by some person or persons unknown ". The decision turned upon the publication to the typist and the question of publication to the blind client does not appear to have been questioned.

(*a*) 1 Mood & R. 258.
(*b*) 1 Ld. Raym. 734.
(*c*) 9 C. & P. 197.
(*d*) 1 De G. & Sm. 314.
(*e*) 9 C. & P. 197, at p. 198.
(*f*) 33 T.L.R. 495.

Workmen's Compensation Acts.

Claims under the Workmen's Compensation Acts in respect of accidents resulting in injury to the sight are not within the scope of this work, but one Scottish case under those Acts is of importance and must be referred to here. It has been held that a blind man employed in the industrial department of an Institute for the Blind is employed under a contract of service within the Workmen's Compensation Acts, and is therefore entitled to compensation for an injury arising out of and in the course of his employment by such Institute.(a)

Negligence.

With regard to negligence, no greater duty is owed to blind persons than to other members of the community, in the absence of notice that they are blind. On the other hand, blind persons injured by the negligence of others are not, by reason of their disability, in any less favourable position for the recovery of damages than other persons.

There are at present no English authorities for these propositions, which rest upon analogy with the position of other disabled persons, for example, the deaf,(b) but they are well illustrated by two decisions of the Court of Session. In *Rennie* v. *Great North of Scotland Railway Co.*(c) an invitation to alight was

(a) *MacGillivray* v. *Northern Counties Institute for the Blind.* [1911] S.C. 897.

(b) See, for example, *R.* v. *Longbottom* (1849), 3 Cox, C.C., 439.

(c) (1905) 12 S.L.T. 667.

given by the servants of a railway company when certain carriages were not drawn up to the platform. A blind man in one of these, hearing other carriage doors being opened, got out, and was seriously injured by falling on to the line.   It was held that the company was negligent in failing to warn passengers to keep their seats, and that the plaintiff was not guilty of contributory negligence merely in that he, being blind, got out of his carriage without assistance on being invited to do so.   In the circumstances, he used reasonable care, and the company, although not subject to any exceptional responsibility towards the blind, were liable to him upon the ordinary principles of the law of negligence.

In *M'Kibbin* v. *Glasgow Corpn.*,(a) again, a partially blind woman stepped into an unguarded hydrant on a street pavement.   In an action against the corporation it was held that the existence of a physical disability in the pursuer did not relieve the corporation of liability for negligence.   In the course of his judgment the Lord Justice Clerk said :(b)

" I demur to the view that blind people are not
" entitled to walk about the streets unless accom-
" panied by some person in charge of them.   I do
" not think that is the law. . . . I do not suggest
" that there is any special duty to the blind of the
" city so far as the condition of the streets is con-
" cerned, but I think that public authorities have
" imposed upon them such a duty as requires

(a) (1920) 57 S.L.R. 476.
(b) 57 S.L.R. 476, at pp. 477, 478.

"them to see that the streets, and the pavements
"particularly, have not open holes in them into
"which either blind people or seeing people may
"stumble and fall without fault on their part."

For the standard of diligence of education authorities towards blind children under their care, see p. 64
post.

Wills.

The testamentary capacity of a blind person was
subject to strict rules in the old Ecclesiastical Courts.
He could make a nuncupative Will by declaring his
Will before a sufficient number of witnesses, but if his
testament was in writing it had to be read over before
witnesses and acknowledged in their presence.(*a*)
This is not the rule in our courts to-day, however.
It was decided in *Longchamp d. Goodfellow* v. *Fish*
(1807)(*b*) that it was not necessary to the validity of a
Will of lands that it should be read over to the testator in the presence of the witnesses.   As Chambre, J.,
said :

"Testators are generally very averse to have
"their intended dispositions of property made
"known in their families before their deaths ; and
"blind men, who stand so much in need of
"attention from their relatives, would probably
"be peculiarly averse to it."(*c*)

(*a*) Swinburne on Wills.
(*b*) 2 Bos. & P.N.R. 415.
(*c*) *Ibid.* at p. 420.

All that is necessary to be proved is that the Will is conformable to the instructions and intentions of the testator.(a)   This may be proved either by evidence that the Will was read over in the presence of witnesses, or in some other way, for example, by the affidavit of one of the attesting witnesses that the testator at the time of execution was aware of the contents of the Will.(b)

Proof of Will.

It is now required by the Probate Rules that before allowing probate of the Will of a blind person to issue the registrar must be satisfied that the Will was read over to the testator before execution, and that he understood it or had knowledge of its contents.   For this purpose an affidavit of due execution will be required.   A form of affidavit may be found in *Mortimer on Probate*, 2nd. Edition, at p. 937.(c)

Attestation of Will.

The Wills Act, 1837 (c.26), section 9, requires a Will to be attested by two witnesses who must sign in the presence of the testator and of each other.   Where the Will is attested in the constructive presence only of the testator, on account of his blindness, it must be shown that the testator was in such a position in

---

(a) *Barton* v. *Robins* (1769) 3 Phill. 455n ; *Fincham* v. *Edwards* (1842) 3 Curt. 63, affd. sub nom. *Edwards* v. *Fincham* (1842) 4 Moo. P.C.C. 198.
(b) *Re Axford* (1860) 1 Sw. & Tr. 540.
(c) Probate Rules (Non-Contentious), 1862, r. 71.

relation to the witnesses that if he had had his sight he could have seen them.(a)

Charities.

As to the position of charities for the blind, apart from legislation, see Chapter 2 *post*.

(a) *In the Goods of Piercy* (1845) 1 Rob. Ecc. 278.

CHAPTER 2.

CHARITIES FOR THE BLIND.

CHARITY has been defined by Lord Macnaghten in the following terms :

"Charity in its legal sense comprises four "principal divisions : trusts for the relief of poverty; "trusts for the advancement of education ; trusts "for the advancement of religion ; and trusts for "other purposes beneficial to the community not "falling under any of the preceding heads."(a)

Bequests for the Blind.

Bequests for the benefit of the Blind have been held to be charitable within this definition. In *Re Fraser, Yeates* v. *Fraser(b)* there was a bequest to trustees for the benefit of the Blind of Invernesshire, and this was accepted as a good charitable gift, the case being argued upon another point. In *Re Elliott, Raven* v. *Nicholson(c)* there was a bequest to

"pay and apply the income of the trust funds

(a) per Lord Macnaghten in *Commissioners for the Special Purposes of Income Tax* v. *Pemsel* [1891] A. C. 531, at p. 583.
(b) (1883) 22 Ch. D. 827.
(c) (1910) 102 L.T. 528.

" exclusively for the maintenance, support, educa-
" tion or otherwise for the benefit of blind persons
" resident in the City of Newcastle or in the county
" borough of Gateshead, only to such blind persons
" as are hereinafter referred to, that is to say, for the
" benefit of blind persons only who, in the opinion of
" my trustees, intend to be honest and industrious,
" my intention being that the payment or applica-
" tion of the income shall not take away the self-
" respect of those blind persons deriving benefit
" therefrom, but shall tend to make them fit for
" work and capable of earning an independent
" living."

The question arising here was whether there was a
sufficient intention to relieve poverty expressed to
make this bequest in a legal sense charitable. Parker
J., held that there was, but in the construction of
future bequests for the Blind of a similar nature it
must be remembered that the Privy Council have laid
it down in 1924, in the case of *Verge* v. *Somerville,* (a)
that a valid charitable trust may exist although in its
administration the benefit is not confined by the
donor to the poor to the exclusion of the rich.

It may now be said that a bequest for the Blind
will be regarded as a charitable gift, as being beneficial to the community within the fourth division of
Pemsel's Case.(b) A similar view has been held in
Australia, where a gift " to the Blind " *simpliciter* has
been held to be a good charitable gift.(c)

(a) [1924] A.C. 496.
(b) See p. 10, *ante.*
(c) *Re Bond, Brennan* v. *Attorney-General* [1929] V.L.R. 333.

Validity of Bequest.

In order to constitute a valid gift the amount given
must be ascertainable and the application to charity
must be obligatory. A gift which is discretionary
only, or which is for alternative charitable or other
purposes does not constitute a valid charitable
bequest.

Construction of Bequest.

Difficult questions of construction may arise
where the object of a charitable bequest is not clear.
Of two possible constructions the one making a
bequest effectual is to be chosen.(a) Parol evidence
may be admitted to ascertain the intended benefici-
ary, where a description applies indifferently to more
than one charity, and the fact that the testator was a
subscriber to, or had an interest in, one of these, will
be a material circumstance.(b)

Misdescription.

Misdescription will not invalidate a gift but the
misdescription may apply to more than one charity.
A bequest to a " County Hospital ", for example, was
held to be intended to apply to a general hospital,
and a county Ophthalmic Hospital could not take.(c)

(a) *Bruce* v. *Deer Presbytery* (1867) L.R. 1 Sc. & Div. 96.
(b) *Re Briscoe's Trusts* (1872) 26 L.T. 149 ; *Re Beale, Beale* v.
Royal Hospital for Incurables (1890) 6 T.L.R. 308.
(c) *Re Alchin's Trusts, Ex p. Furley, Ex p. Rommey (Earl)*
(1872) L.R. 14 Eq. 230.

A gift to the "Westminster Hospital Charing Cross", again, was held to apply to the Charing Cross Hospital and not the Westminster Ophthalmic Hospital.(a)   The inclusion of the specific name of the secretary may be a deciding factor.(b)

In the case of a gift to " Soldiers Crippled Homes ", the legacy was divided between three institutions in the absence of evidence that the testatrix knew about any of the claimants.(c)

Change of Name and Amalgamation.

Where an institution has changed its name since the Will it will still take, and where it has amalgamated with another to which a bequest is also made, the united society may take both legacies.(d)   In the case of a gift to a local branch of an institution the central institution has been held entitled on construction of its by-laws,(e) and also where the central institution has amalgamated with the local branch.(f)   A gift to a closed branch of a hospital may be a gift to the hospital generally.(g)   Indeed, wherever a named institution has ceased to exist at the death of the testator an institution in existence

---

(a) *Bradshaw* v. *Thompson* (1843) 2 Y. & C. Ch. Cas. 295.
(b) *Re Morgan, Marriott* v. *Society for the Abolition of Vivisection* (1909) 25 T.L.R. 303.
(c) *Re Husband, Neave* v. *Barnardo's Homes National Incorporated Association* (1923) 58 L. Jo. 600.
(d) *Re Joy, Purday* v. *Johnson* (1888) 60 L.T. 175.
(e) *Royal National Lifeboat Institution* v. *Turver* (1915) 31 T.L.R. 340.
(f) *Re Marchant, Weaver* v. *Royal Society for the Prevention of Cruelty to Animals* (1910) 54 Sol. Jo. 425.
(g) *Re Bradfield* (1892) 8 T.L.R. 696.

with a similar name and objects may take,(a) but
not where the testator intends to benefit a specific
institution and not to make a general charitable gift.
Thus, a legacy to an Ophthalmic hospital which had
ceased to exist at the date of the testator's Will was
held to have lapsed, Pearson, J., saying :

> "I certainly come to the conclusion that his
> "object as far as regards the Blind, was not to give
> "general legacies for the benefit of blind persons but
> "to give particular legacies for particular institu-
> "tions established for the care, protection or educa-
> "tion of the Blind and that instead of picking out
> "one general object, namely, blind persons, he
> "meant to pick out particular institutions which
> "he thought worthy of encouragement."(b)

Income Tax.

The Inland Revenue also take the view that a
bequest for the Blind is a charitable gift, for charities
for the Blind are generally exempt from the payment
of income tax as charities within *Pemsel's Case* or
as charities registered under the Blind Persons Act,
1920 (c. 49). The exemptions from income tax granted
to charities generally are contained in the Income
Tax Act, 1918 (c. 40), section 37; the Finance Act,
1921 (c. 32), section 30 ; and the Finance Act, 1927
(c. 10), section 24.

(a) *Re Magrath, Histed* v. *Queen's University of Belfast* [1913]
2 Ch. 331.
(b) *Re Ovey, Broadbent* v. *Barrow* (1885) 29 Ch. D. 560, at p. 563.

Exemption from Schedule A.

Exemption from tax under Schedule A. is granted in respect of the rents and profits of any lands, tenements, hereditaments, or heritages vested in trustees for charitable purposes so far as the same are applied to charitable purposes only.(a) This exemption now extends to lands, tenements, hereditaments, and heritages owned and occupied by a charity,(b) which means any body of persons or trust established for charitable purposes only.(c) The exemption does not apply in respect of rent payable or other annual payment to be made by a charity in respect of lands, tenements, hereditaments, or heritages which are in the use and enjoyment of a person whose total income from all sources amounts to not less than one hundred and fifty pounds.(d)

Exemption from Schedule B.

Exemption from tax under Schedule B. is granted in respect of lands occupied by a charity. (e) This exemption does not apply in the case of lands which are occupied for the purpose of husbandry unless the work in connection with the husbandry is mainly carried on by beneficiaries of the charity and the profits, if any, arising therefrom are applied solely

---

(a) Income Tax Act, 1918 (c. 40), s. 37 (1) (a).
(b) Finance Act, 1921 (c. 32), s. 30 (1) (a).
(c) *Ibid,* s. 30 (3).
(d) *Ibid.* s. 30 (2).
(e) *Ibid.* s. 30 (1) (b).

to the purposes of the charity.(*a*)   Nor does it apply where the lands are in the use and enjoyment of a person whose total income from all sources amounts to not less than one hundred and fifty pounds.(*b*) Charity means any body of persons or trust established for charitable purposes only.(*c*)

Exemption from Schedule C.

Exemption from tax under Schedule C. is granted in respect of any interest, annuities, dividends, or shares of annuities, and from tax under Schedule D. in respect of any yearly interest or other annual payment forming part of the income of any body of persons or trust established for charitable purposes only, or which, according to the rules and regulations established by Act of Parliament, charter, decree, deed of trust, or Will, are applicable to charitable purposes only.(*d*)

Exemption from Schedule D.

Exemption from tax under Schedule D. is granted as set out in the last paragraph, and, in addition, exemption is granted in respect of the profits of a trade carried on by any charity; if the profits are applied solely to the purposes of the charity and either :—

(*a*) Finance Act, 1921 (c. 32), s. 30 (1) (b).
(*b*) *Ibid.* s. 30 (2).
(*c*) *Ibid.* s. 30 (3).
(*d*) Income Tax Act, 1918 (c. 40), s. 37 (1) (b).

(i) the trade is exercised in the course of the actual carrying out of a primary purpose of the charity ; or

(ii) the work in connection with the trade is mainly carried on by beneficiaries of the charity.(a)

Charity means any body of persons or trust established for charitable purposes only.(b)

Charities within Blind Persons Act.

Charities for the Blind are subject to the provisions of the Blind Persons Act, 1920 (c. 49), which incorporates with modifications the War Charities Act, 1916 (c. 43).(c) For the purposes of the Act, a charity for the Blind is any fund, institution or association, (whether established before or after the commencement of the Act) which has, or professes to have, for its object, or one of its objects, the provision of assistance in any form to blind persons, or any other charitable purpose relating to blind persons.   Where this object is subsidiary to the principal purposes of the charity, however, the fund, institution, or association is not within the scope of the definition.(d)

Every charity for the Blind within the foregoing definition is prohibited from raising money from the public unless it is first registered.(e)   An organisation which is in fact a charity, and is certified to be such by the Charity Commissioners, is not absolved

---

(a) Finance Act, 1927 (c. 10), s. 24.
(b) Finance Act, 1921 (c. 32), s. 30 (3).
(c) Blind Persons Act, 1920 (c. 49), s. 3.
(d) Ibid., s. 3 (3).
(e) War Charities Act, 1916 (c. 43), s. 1 (1).

L. R. B.   C

from the requirement of registration by reason of the
fact that it is also a trade union registered under the
Trade Union Act.(*a*)

Administration of Blind Persons Act.

The administration of the Blind Persons Act, as of
the War Charities Act, is in the hands of the Charity
Commissioners, and, subject to their control, the
local registration authorities.   In order to effect the
carrying out of the Act the Charity Commissioners
are given power to make Regulations(*b*) which are
subject to the approval of the Ministry of Health.(*c*)
The matters in respect of which Regulations may be
made are the following(*d*) :—

(a) the forms of application and the particulars to
be contained therein.

(b) the form of the registers to be kept under the
Act and the particulars to be entered therein.

(c) provision for inspection of registers and lists,
and for making and furnishing and certification
of copies and extracts.

(d) fees in respect of registration, copies and extracts.

(e) notification of changes requiring alteration of
particulars in the register.

(f) exemption of charities from the requirements of
the Act, and the grounds therefor.

(g) any other matters necessary for carrying the
Act into effect.

(*a*) *Barber* v. *Chudley* (1922) 92 L.J.K.B. 711.
(*b*) War Charities Act, 1916 (c. 43), s. 4.
(*c*) Blind Persons Act, 1920 (c. 49), s. 3 (1) (d).
(*d*) War Charities Act, 1916 (c. 43), s. 4.

Regulations have been made by the Charities for the Blind Regulations, 1920.(*a*) The effect of these Regulations is given where relevant to the subject matter in the succeeding pages.

Registration of Charities.

The provisions relating to registration are contained in the War Charities Act, 1916 (c. 43), and in Regulations made by the Charity Commissioners under the powers given to them by the War Charities Act, and approved by the Ministry of Health.(*b*) Application for registration is to be made to the registration authority for the area in which the administrative centre of the charity is situated.   In case of doubt as to where such centre is situated, the question is to be finally decided by the Charity Commissioners.(*c*)

Local Branches.

With regard to local branches of, or local committees or bodies affiliated to, Central Organisations. which are already registered, the necessity for registration of such branches, etc. is dependent upon the question of whether the Central Organisation is wholly responsible for the administration of such branches, etc.   If full responsibility so rests, then the branches are merely local agents and do not require separate registration, but in such a case it is necessary

---

(*a*) S.R. & O. 1920, No. 1696.
(*b*) War Charities Act, 1916 (c. 43), s. 4.
(*c*) Ibid., s. 2 (2).

that full accounts of all receipts and expenditure should be forwarded to the Central Organisation, who are responsible for any improper administration.(*a*)

Registration Authorities.

The registration authority to which application is to be made is, in the City of London, the Common Council of the City of London, and elsewhere, the county council or county borough council.(*b*) The London County Council is, in practice, the registration authority for the larger charities and in particular the National charities, since all these have their administrative centres in London.

A council may act through a committee, which may include persons, including women, who are not members of the council.(*c*)

Application for Registration.

Application must be made on Form B. 4., obtainable from the Charity Commissioners, and must be signed by some person or persons duly authorised on behalf of the Charity.(*d*)

The fee payable to the registration authority on application is one guinea.(*e*) Any question whether a charity is a charity for the Blind is a question of

---

(*a*) Memorandum on Blind Persons Act (B. 2), para. 9 (4).
(*b*) Blind Persons Act, 1920 (c. 49), s. 3 (1) (a).
(*c*) War Charities Act, 1916 (c. 43), s. 2 (1), proviso.
(*d*) S.R. & O. 1920, No. 1696, r. 3.
(*e*) *Ibid.*, r. 8.

fact,(a) to be finally decided by the Charity Commissioners.(b) An application to determine the question may be made by the Charity or by the registration authority. It must be made on Form B. 6, obtainable from the Charity Commissioners, signed by some person or persons duly authorised on behalf of the Charity or authority, and must be accompanied by full information as to the objects and constitution of the Charity.(c)

Refusal to Register.

Registration must be granted by the registration authority after making such inquiries as they may think fit. They have no discretion to refuse to register a Charity whose administrative centre is within their area unless they are satisfied :—

(1) that the charity is not established in good faith for charitable purposes ;(d) or
(2) that it will not comply with the conditions imposed by the War Charities Act ;(e) or
(3) that it will not be properly administered ;(f) or
(4) that its objects are adequately attained by another charity registered under the War Charities Act.(g)

(a) *Barber* v. *Chudley* (1922) 92 L.J.K.B. 711, at p. 713.
(b) War Charities Act, 1916 (c. 43), s. 10.
(c) S.R. & O., 1920, No. 1696, r. 20.
(d) War Charities Act, 1916 (c. 43), s. 2 (3).
(e) *Ibid.*
(f) *Ibid.*
(g) Blind Persons Act, 1920 (c. 49), s. 3 (1) (b).

Conditions Precedent to Registration.

The conditions with which a charity is required to comply to entitle it to registration are the following :

(1) the charity must be administered by a responsible committee or other body consisting of not less than three persons.(a)

(2) the Chairman, Secretary, Treasurer, and Auditor must have been appointed, for these must appear in the register kept by the registration authority. The first three offices may be held by members of the committee, or by the same person. The Auditor must be a person approved by the registration authority.(b)

(3) The bank at which the account of the charity is kept must have been selected; this also appears in the register. The Charity Commissioners consider that this should be an institution coming within the following definition :—" The Post Office Savings Bank or ' any Savings Bank certified under the Act of 1863 ', or any institution which in the ordinary course of its business honours cheques drawn upon it by persons from and for whom it receives moneys on current account."(c)

(4) Minutes of meetings of the committee or other body must be kept, in which must be recorded the names of members attending.(d)

(a) War Charities Act, 1916 (c. 43), s. 3 (i).
(b) Memorandum on Blind Persons Act (B. 2), para. 9 (1).
(c) Ibid., para. 9 (2).
(d) War Charities Act, 1916 (c. 43), s. 3 (i.)

(5) Proper books of accounts must be kept and such accounts must include the total receipts and total expenditure of any collection, bazaar, sale, entertainment, or exhibition held with the approval of the governing body of the charity.(*a*)

(6) The accounts must be audited at such intervals as may be prescribed by Regulations under the Act by some person or persons approved by the registration authority, and copies of the accounts so audited must be sent to the registration authority.(*b*) It is accordingly provided that duly audited accounts must be sent to the registration authority at least once in every twelve months.(*c*) The registration authority, may, however, with the consent of the Charity Commissioners, or the Charity Commissioners may themselves, call for accounts at any time.(*d*) Accounts so sent need relate only to receipt and expenditure of money, but every registered charity is further required by this regulation to keep a sufficient record of all dealings in kind, of whatever nature.(*e*)

(7) Every account must be kept in the name of the charity.(*f*)

(8) All moneys received by the charity must be paid into a separate account at such bank or

---

(*a*) War Charities Act, 1916 (c. 43), s. 3 (ii).
(*b*) *Ibid.*
(*c*) S.R. & O. 1920, No. 1696, r. 13.
(*d*) *Ibid.*
(*e*) *Ibid.*
(*f*) *Ibid.*, r. 9.

banks as may be specified as respects the charity in the register.(*a*)

(9) Such particulars of accounts and other records as the registration authority or the Charity Commissioners may require must be furnished to the registration authority or the Charity Commissioners.(*b*)

(10) The books and accounts of the charity must be open to inspection at any time by any person duly authorised by the registration authority or the Charity Commissioners.(*c*)

Observance of Conditions.

Every person who is for the time being a member of the committee of the registered charity is responsible for the observance of these conditions. If they are not observed every person so responsible is liable on summary conviction to a fine not exceeding £100, or to imprisonment with or without hard labour for a term not exceeding three months.(*d*)

Grant of Registration.

On grant of registration a certificate of registration in the prescribed form, Form B. 10, must be given to the charity by the registration authority.(*e*)

(*a*) War Charities Act, 1916 (c. 43), s. 3 (iii).
(*b*) Ibid., s. 3 (iv).
(*c*) Ibid.
(*d*) Ibid., s. 9 (1) ; Blind Persons Act, 1920 (c. 49), s. 3 (1) (f) ;
     S.R. & O. 1920, No. 1696, r. 19.
(*e*) War Charities Act, 1916 (c. 43), s. 2 (5).

Appeal from Refusal to Register.

If the registration authority should refuse to register a charity the applicant is not without a remedy.   In such a case an appeal lies to the Charity Commissioners.(a)   The appeal must be made in writing within fourteen days from the date of the intimation of the refusal to register, or within such further time as may be allowed by the Charity Commissioners.(b)   A statement giving the reasons for the appeal must accompany it, together with any evidence in support which the appellants may desire to adduce.(c)   Notice of appeal must be given at the same time to the registration authority.(d)   The authority must forthwith communicate to the Charity Commissioners their reasons for refusing registration and the evidence in support of such reasons.(e)

Hearing of Appeal.

For the purposes of this appeal, the Charity Commissioners have all such powers as are exercisable by them under the Charitable Trusts Acts, 1853-1914, with regard to requiring accounts, statements, written answers to enquiries, the attendance of persons for examination on oath or otherwise, the production of documents, the furnishing of copies and

---

(a) War Charities Act, 1916 (c. 43), s. 2 (4).
(b) S.R. & O., 1920, No. 1696, r. 14.
(c) Ibid.
(d) Ibid., r. 15.
(e) Ibid.

extracts from documents, the examination of registers and records, and the transmission of documents for examination.(*a*)

If, as a result of the appeal, the Charity Commissioners come to the conclusion that registration ought not to be refused, the registration authority must register the charity.(*b*)

Register of Charities.

Every registration authority is required to keep a register of the charities registered by them.(*c*) This register must contain the following particulars(*d*) :—

(a) The name of the charity.

(b) Date of establishment.

(c) The precise objects of the charity.

(d) The address of the administrative centre of the charity. Where application for registration is made by the local branch of an organisation the address to be entered is that of the local branch and not that of the headquarters of the organisation. A mistake in this respect invalidates the registration.(*e*)

(e) The name and address of the Secretary.

(f) The name and address of the Treasurer.

(g) The full names, addresses, and descriptions of the Chairman and the other members of the Committee.

(*a*) War Charities Act, 1916 (c. 43), s. 6.
(*b*) *Ibid.*, s. 2 (4).
(*c*) *Ibid.*, s. 2 (5).
(*d*) S.R. & O. 1920, No. 1696, r. 4.
(*e*) Memorandum on Blind Persons Act (B. 2), para. 9 (3).

(h) The name and address of the bank or banks at which the account of the charity is kept.
(i) The name and address of the Auditor.
(j) The date of application for registration.
(k) The date of registration.
(l) (if a charity be removed from the register) the date of removal.

A duplicate of the entries relating to each registered charity must be entered by the registration authority on a separate sheet, which must be sent forthwith to the Charity Commissioners. A supply of these sheets is obtainable from the Charity Commissioners on application for Form B. 7.(a)

List of Charities refused Registration.

The registration authority is also required to keep lists of charities which have been refused registration.(b) The particulars which such lists must contain are the following(c) :—

(a) The name of the charity.
(b) The address of the administrative centre of the charity. Where application for registration is made by the local branch of an organisation the address to be entered is that of the local branch and not that of the headquarters of the organisation. A mistake in this respect invalidates the registration.(d)
(c) The precise objects of the charity.

(a) S.R. & O. 1920, No. 1696, r. 5.
(b) War Charities Act, 1916 (c. 43), s. 2 (5).
(c) S.R. & O. 1920, No. 1696, r. 6.
(d) Memorandum on Blind Persons Act (B. 2), para. 9 (3).

(d) The name, address, and description of each
person applying on behalf of the charity for
registration or exemption.

(e) The considerations which have led the authority to refuse registration or to exempt the
charity from registration.

(f) The date on which consent of the Minister of
Health to exemption was given.

(g) The date of refusal or exemption.

(h) The specified period, if any, for which exemption was granted.

A duplicate of the entries relating to each charity
refused registration, or exempted from registration,
must be entered in a separate List Sheet, which must
be sent forthwith to the Charity Commissioners. A
supply of these sheets is obtainable from the Charity
Commissioners on application for Form B. 8 or
B. 9.(a)

Alteration of Register.

Any changes in the particulars supplied for entry
in the register must be at once communicated to the
registration authority, who must make the necessary
alteration in the register, and immediately notify the
same to the Charity Commissioners.(b)

Inspection of Register.

The register and lists are open to the inspection of
all persons free of charge. Persons interested may

(a) S.R. & O. 1920, No. 1696, r. 7.
(b) Ibid., r. 10.

make copies of, or extracts from, any entry relating to a specific charity, on payment of a fee of three-pence. Copies and extracts are supplied to persons interested on payment of a fee of sixpence for each copy or extract. When they are obtained from the registration authority they are certified by the signature of the clerk to the registration authority, or of some person authorised to act on his behalf when the copies or extracts are obtained ; when they are obtained from the Charity Commissioners they are certified by the signature of the Secretary to the Commissioners or some person authorised on his behalf.(a)

Combined Register.

The Charity Commissioners are required to keep a combined register of all charities registered under the Act, and two combined lists, the one comprising all charities of which registration has been refused, and the other comprising all charities which have been exempted from registration.(b)

Expenses.

Expenses incurred by the London County Council acting as registration authority are to be defrayed out of the county fund as expenses for general county purposes. Expenses incurred by any other county council, or by the Common Council of the City of London, or by a county borough council as registration

(a) S.R. & O. 1920, No. 1696, r. 12.
(b) War Charities Act, 1916 (c. 43), s. 2 (6).

authority may be paid out of any fund or rate out of which the expenses of the council are payable.(a)

Public Appeals.

In the absence of registration in accordance with the foregoing provisions it is illegal to make any appeal to the public for donations or subscriptions in money or in kind for a charity which is within the definition of a charity for the Blind, or to raise money for any such charity by promoting any bazaar, sale, entertainment or exhibition, or by any similar means. Further, the approval in writing of the committee or other governing body of the charity must be obtained, either directly or through any person duly authorised to give such approval on behalf of such governing body.(b) The committee may impose conditions in giving this approval. One of these conditions must be that an account of all receipts and expenditure in connection with the bazaar, sale, entertainment or exhibition, shall be rendered to them.(c)

All posters, bills, circulars, advertisements, and notices relating to every such appeal to the public or attempt to raise money must contain the name of the charity in full as appearing on the certificate of registration, together with the words, " Registered under the Blind Persons Act, 1920."(d)

A breach of these requirements is an offence

(a) War Charities Act, 1916 (c. 43), s. 2 (7), (8).
(b) Ibid., s. 1 (1).
(c) S.R. & O. 1920, No. 1696, r. 17.
(d) Ibid., r. 18.

carrying with it a liability on summary conviction to a fine not exceeding £100 or to imprisonment with or without hard labour for a term not exceeding three months.(a)   It is not necessary that there should be *mala fides* or dishonest intent.(b)

The provisions of the Blind Persons Act do not apply to any collection at Divine service, nor to a charity which has been exempted from compliance with the Act.(c)

Exemption from Registration.

A charity may apply to the registration authority for the area in which the administrative centre of the charity is situated, for exemption from registration under the Act.   Every application must be on Form B. 5, obtainable from the Charity Commissioners, and must be signed by some person or persons duly authorised on behalf of the charity.(d)

Exemption may be granted if in the opinion of the registration authority the scope of the operations of the charity as regards the amount of the subscriptions expected to be received, the duration of the charity or the area of collection or of benefit is so limited as to make it unnecessary in the interests of the public that the charity should be registered.(e)

The decision of the registration authority is subject to the control of the Ministry of Health, whose

---

(a) War Charities Act, 1916 (c. 43), s. 9 (1).
(b) *Barber* v. *Chudley* (1922) 92 L.J.K.B. 711.
(c) War Charities Act, 1916 (c. 43), s. 1 (1) proviso.
(d) S.R. & O. 1920, No. 1696, r. 3.
(e) *Ibid.*, r. 16 (1).

consent is necessary to a grant of exemption.(a)
No appeal lies from the refusal of a registration
authority to grant exemption from registration.

The exemption may be limited to such period of
time as may be determined by the registration authority, again subject to the consent of the Ministry
of Health.(b)

A certificate of exemption must be given to any
charity exempted, in the statutory form, Form
B. 11.(c)

The grant of exemption is liable to be withdrawn
if at any time the registration authority should consider that the character of an exempted charity has
materially varied in any of the respects which in-
duced the grant of exemption. The registration
authority must obtain the consent of the Ministry
of Health to such withdrawal.(d)

Removal from Register.

Although a charity for the Blind has been registered
it can subsequently be removed from the register
by the registration authority on certain grounds.
These are :—

(a) That it is not being carried on in good faith for
   charitable purposes ; or
(b) That it is not complying with any of the conditions imposed by the Act ; or
(c) That it is not being properly administered.(e)

(a) S.R. & O. 1920, No. 1696, r. 16 (1).
(b) *Ibid.*, r. 16 (2).
(c) War Charities Act, 1916 (c. 43), s. 2 (5).
(d) S.R. & O. 1920, No. 1696, r. 16 (3).
(e) War Charities Act, 1916 (c. 43), s. 5 (1).

Notice of such removal must be given to the public and to the Charity Commissioners,(a) together with full particulars of the reason for the removal, and all information in the possession of the authority in regard to the funds and securities of the charity, and the persons holding them.(b)

The Charity Commissioners have power to make certain orders on removal of a charity from the register.   These are :—

(a) An order to any bank or other person who holds money or securities on behalf of the charity not to part with such money or securities without the authority of the Commissioners.

(b) An order for payment or transfer to the Official Trustee of Charitable Funds of any cash or securities held for the charity, and for that purpose they may make, without any application to them for the purpose, any such order as they are authorised to make under section 2 of the Charitable Trusts Act, 1860 (c. 136).(c)

Failure to comply with any of these orders constitutes an offence against the Act, and the person failing to comply is liable on summary conviction to a fine not exceeding £100, or to imprisonment with or without hard labour for a term not exceeding three months.(d)

The Charity Commissioners have also power, on

(a) War Charities Act, 1916 (c. 43), s. 5 (1).
(b) S.R. & O. 1920, No. 1696, r. 11.
(c) War Charities Act, 1916 (c. 43), s. 5 (2).
(d) Ibid., ss. 5 (2), 9 (1).

L. R. B.

D

removal of a charity from the register, to establish
a scheme for the regulation of the charity in accordance with their ordinary jurisdiction under the Charitable Trusts Acts, 1853 to 1914, as if the charity
were a charity within the jurisdiction of the Commissioners under those Acts. No special application
need be made for the exercise of this power.(a)

Appeal against Removal.

An appeal lies to the Charity Commissioners
against a decision to remove a charity from the
register.(b) The appeal must be made in writing
within fourteen days from the date of the intimation
of the intention to remove, or within such further
time as may be allowed by the Commissioners.(c)
A statement giving the reasons for the appeal must
accompany it, together with any evidence in support
which the appellants may desire to adduce.(d)
Notice of appeal must be given at the same time to
the registration authority. The authority must
forthwith communicate to the Commissioners their
reasons for deciding to remove the charity, and the
evidence in support of such reasons.(e)

Hearing of Appeal.

For the purposes of the appeal the Charity Commissioners have all such powers as are exercisable

---

(a) War Charities Act, 1916, (c. 43), s. 5 (3).
(b) *Ibid.*, s. 5 (1), proviso.
(c) S.R. & O. 1920, No. 1696, r. 14.
(d) *Ibid.*
(e) *Ibid.*, r. 15.

by them under the Charitable Trusts Acts, 1853 to 1914, with regard to requiring accounts, statements, written answers to inquiries, the attendance of persons for examination on oath or otherwise, the production of documents, the furnishing of copies and extracts from documents, the examination of registers and records, and the transmission of documents for examination.(a)

Offences under Blind Persons Act.

Offences in connection with the Blind Persons Act consist of :—

(a) Failure to observe the conditions entitling the charity to registration.(b)

(b) Raising money from the public otherwise than in conformity with the Act.(c)

(c) Disobedience to an order of the Charity Commissioners in regard to money or securities.(d)

(d) Making any false statement or false representation in an application for registration or exemption, or in any notification of any change requiring alteration in the registered particulars.(e)

(e) False representation of being an officer or agent of a charity for the Blind.(f)

(f) Failure to send any notification required to be sent.(g)

(a) War Charities Act, 1916 (c. 43), s. 6; Blind Persons Act, 1920 (c. 49), s. 3 (1) (e).
(b) See p. 22, *ante.*
(c) See p. 30, *ante.*
(d) See p. 33, *ante.*
(e) War Charities Act, 1916 (c. 43), s. 8.
(f) *Ibid.*
(g) *Ibid.*

The penalty for these offences is on summary conviction a fine not exceeding £100, or imprisonment with or without hard labour for a term not exceeding three months.(a)

The consent of the Charity Commissioners is necessary to the commencement of all proceedings for an offence under the Act.(b)

Powers over Unregistered Charities.

The Charity Commissioners have also important powers in relation to unregistered charities for the blind,(c) irrespective of whether application in respect of them has or has not been made, or, having been made, has been refused.(d)   In any case, where the Charity Commissioners are satisfied on the representation of a registration authority or of a Chief Officer of Police that there is reasonable ground for believing that a charity for the Blind

(a) is not being or has not been carried on in good faith for charitable purposes, or

(b) is not complying or has not complied with conditions substantially corresponding with the conditions imposed on registered charities under the Act, or

(c) is not being or has not been properly administered, the Charity Commissioners may exercise as respects the charity any of the powers

---

(a) War Charities Act, 1916 (c. 43), s. 9 (1).
(b) Ibid., s. 9 (2).
(c) War Charities Act, 1916 (c. 43), s. 7 (1).
(d) Ibid., s. 7 (2).

which are exercisable by them with respect to a charity which, having been registered under the Act, has been removed from the register,(a) except that they may not exercise the power of establishing a scheme for the regulation of a charity without giving the charity a full opportunity of being heard.(b)

For the purpose of an inquiry into any charity in this regard the Charity Commissioners have the same powers in relation to the charity as are conferred on the Commissioners for the purpose of appeals.(c)

(a) See p. 33, *ante*.
(b) War Charities Act, 1916 (c. 43), s. 7 (1).
(c) See p. 35, *ante*.

CHAPTER 3.

THE WELFARE OF THE BLIND.

IT is now recognised that the welfare of the Blind is the concern of the community as a whole, and should no longer be left solely to voluntary organisations. The department of Government primarily concerned with this matter is the Ministry of Health, but the actual administration is in the hands of the Local Authorities acting in conjunction with the voluntary agencies. A Departmental Committee on the Welfare of the Blind was set up by Sir Herbert Samuel as President of the Local Government Board in 1914. It reported in 1917, and as a consequence an Advisory Committee on the Blind was appointed, and a system of Exchequer grants to Local Authorities introduced, in respect of various services for the Blind. The whole system of these Exchequer grants was altered by the Local Government Act, 1929 - (c. 17), and the present position is detailed at length, *infra*.

Definition of Blind.

The definition of " blind " suggested by the Departmental Committee, and adopted by the Ministry of Health is " too blind to perform work for which eyesight is essential ". This definition is substantially the same as that in the Blind Persons Act, 1920 (c. 49), section 1,(a) but is considerably narrower than that in the Education Act, 1921 (c. 51), section 69.(b)

In interpreting this definition persons with a visual acuity greater than 6/60ths (Snellen) with the most suitable glasses are regarded as not being blind, in the absence of special conditions such as nystagmus or great contraction of the field of vision. Consideration must be given to all the visual conditions, but not to other bodily or mental infirmities.(c)

The foregoing interpretation is based on a report of the ophthalmological section of the Royal Society of Medicine, dated July 21st, 1915, the revelant portion of which is in the following terms :—

" Experience shows that persons whose acuity " of vision (refractive error being corrected) is below " *one-twentieth* of the normal (3/60ths, Snellen) are " usually unable to perform work requiring eye-" sight, while persons with vision better than *one-* " *tenth* (6/60ths, Snellen) are usually able to " perform some such work. Persons with inter-" mediate degrees may or may not be able ; much " depends on intelligence and bodily strength, and " much on the nature of the blindness.

" A person whose so-called blindness depends on " defects in the centre of the visual field may fail " to reach a given standard, and yet be able to

(a) See p. 60, *post.*
(b) See p. 63, *post.*
(c) Ministry of Health Circular 681 (1926) ; Circular 780 (1927).

" perform some kinds of work requiring eyesight,
" while another person suffering from great con-
" traction of the field of vision may surpass the
" same standard, and yet be unable to walk alone,
" or to do any kind of work requiring eyesight."

Exchequer Contribution for Welfare of the Blind.

As has been said, a system of Exchequer grants for
the welfare of the Blind was introduced in 1918.
Regulations governing these were embodied in Circular 7 B.D. of the Ministry of Health, and although
these ceased to have effect after March 31st, 1930,
they are still of considerable importance as a guide
to Local Authorities.(a) Specific grants were abolished
in 1929 (b) and a General Exchequer Contribution in
respect of various services was substituted.   Out of
this contributions are made by each Local Authority
to the voluntary associations in its area which provide services for the Blind.   The General Exchequer
Contribution is revised periodically and before the
beginning of each fixed grant period a scheme must
be made by the Minister of Health after consultation
with the county councils and county borough councils concerned, or with the associations representing
those councils.   This scheme must provide for payment of contributions of such amounts as may be
specified in the scheme to any voluntary associations
providing services for the welfare of the Blind, by the
councils of counties and county boroughs in which

(a) See Appendix IV.
(b) Local Government Act, 1929 (c. 17), s. 85.

are resident blind persons for whose benefit such services are provided.(*a*)

In the City of London the Common Council is for this purpose to be regarded as the council of a county borough.(*b*)

The Minister has power to alter or revoke any scheme.(*c*)   Alteration is only necessary where substantial change of circumstances occurs, *e.g.*, where the work of a voluntary association is taken over by a Local Authority ; where an association ceases to function ; or where any branch of the work of an association is transferred to another association.(*d*)

The contribution of the council towards the expenses of the voluntary associations under a scheme may be paid directly to the association out of the amount payable as the General Exchequer Grant of the council, upon application being made to the Minister of Health for this purpose.(*e*)   This provision is especially suitable to national services, since the collection of small amounts from numerous authorities would be highly inconvenient.(*f*)

Reduction of Grant.

A council is liable to have its grant reduced if the Minister of Health is satisfied on the representation of any association or body interested that the council have failed to achieve or maintain a reasonable

(*a*) Local Government Act, 1929 (c. 17), s. 102 (1).
(*b*) *Ibid.*
(*c*) *Ibid.*, s. 131 (2).
(*d*) Ministry of Health Circular 1086 (1930).
(*e*) Local Government Act, 1929 (c. 17), s. 106.
(*f*) Ministry of Health Circular 1086 (1930).

standard of efficiency or progress in the discharge of
their functions relating to public health services,
which expression includes the welfare of the Blind,(a)
and that the health or welfare of the inhabitants of
the area of the council or some of them has been, or
is likely to be thereby endangered. Regard is to be
had to the standards maintained in other areas whose
financial resources and other relevant circumstances
are substantially similar.(b)

Schemes and Contributions by Local Authorities.

Schemes have been made in accordance with the
Act, and the present scheme is known as the Welfare
of the Blind (Contributions) Scheme, 1933. This
came into operation on April 1st, 1933, and con-
tinues in force until March 31st, 1937. The scheme
fixes the amount of the contributions payable to
voluntary associations, and to the National Institute
for the Blind, and provides for the disposition of the
sum in the hands of the National Institute for the
benefit of the national services.

Conditions of Contribution to Voluntary Association.

The contributions are annual and must be paid in
equal quarterly instalments in each of the financial
years 1933–34, 1934–35, 1935–36, 1936–37. The
conditions of payment of a contribution to a voluntary association are as follows :—

(a) Local Government Act, 1929 (c. 17), s. 134.
(b) Ibid., s. 104.

(1) The council must be satisfied as to the efficiency of the services provided by the association for the welfare of the Blind in respect of which this contribution is payable.

(2) No reduction or alteration of the services may be made without the consent of the council. It may be made a condition of such consent that a suitable reduction shall be made in the annual contribution payable to the association.

(3) The services and any premises on which the services are carried on must be open to inspection at all reasonable times by an officer of the council duly authorised by the council and by any officer of the Ministry of Health appointed for that purpose by the Minister of Health.

(4) The association must send to the council and to the Minister in each year a copy of the annual report of the association on its work for the welfare of the Blind during the previous year, together with a statement of the accounts of the association for that year relating to such work in the form prescribed by the Minister on December 21st, 1921, (a) or in such other form as the Minister may from time to time direct, and a copy of the auditor's certificate and report, if any, thereon. The association must also furnish the council from time to time with such other information relating to the services for the welfare of the Blind provided by the associa-

---

(a) See Ministry of Health Circular 262 (1921); for new Form of Workshop and Trading Account, see Ministry of Health Circular 1306 (1933).

tion and the expenditure thereon as the council may reasonably require.

Conditions of Contribution to National Institute.

The conditions of payment of contributions to the National Institute are as follows :—

(1) The National Institute for the Blind must distribute the total amount of the contributions received in each year in the manner prescribed in Schedule III of the scheme, that is, among associations providing national services. These are, the National Institute itself : the National Library for the Blind : the British and Foreign Bible Society : the Society for the Promotion of Christian Knowledge : and the College of Teachers of the Blind.

(2) The Minister must be satisfied as to the efficiency of the services for the welfare of the Blind provided by each of the associations in Schedule III.

(3) No reduction or alteration of the services may be made without the consent of the Minister.

(4) Such services and any premises in which those services are carried on must be open to inspection at all reasonable times by any officer of the Ministry of Health appointed for that purpose by the Minister.

(5) Each of the associations must send to the Minister in each year a copy of the annual report of the association on its work for the welfare of the Blind during the previous year, together with a statement of the accounts of the association for

that year relating to such work in the form prescribed by the Minister on December 21st, 1921, (a) or in such other form as the Minister may from time to time direct, and a copy of the auditor's certificate and report, if any, thereon. The Minister must also be furnished from time to time with such other information relating to services provided by the association for the welfare of the Blind and the expenditure thereon as the Minister may reasonably require.

Disputes.

Any dispute or difference between a council and an association in connection with any matter arising out of the scheme is to be referred to the Minister, whose decision is to be final and binding upon the council and the association. No decision is to affect an instalment payable earlier than a month before the reference.

National Services.

Supervision of the national services, *i.e.*, the production of embossed literature and the conduct of the examination for the Home Teacher's Certificate by the College of Teachers, remains with the Ministry of Health. Supervision of all other services is in the hands of the Local Authorities, subject to the Minister being satisfied from time to time that the efficiency and progress of the arrangements is maintained.

(a) See Ministry of Health Circular 262 (1921); for new Form of Workshop and Trading Account, see Ministry of Health Circular 1306 (1933).

Services for the Blind.

The services for the Blind contemplated in the scheme are those indicated in the former Regulations governing Exchequer grants and embodied in Circular 7 B.D. of the Ministry of Health (a) and comprise :—

(1) *Workshops for the Blind.* A "workshop employee" is defined as a blind person who is regularly employed by an approved agency in or about a workshop for the Blind, and in receipt of weekly pay at the trade union or other standard rate customary in the particular class of work on which the blind person is employed, and who is not a pupil undergoing training or an apprentice. In Scotland such an employee has been held to be employed under a contract of service within the Workmen's Compensation Acts.(b)

(2) *Provision of Assistance to Home Workers.* "Home Workers" means adult blind persons who, for sufficient reasons, are employed elsewhere than in a workshop in occupations usually practised in workshops and are attached for the purposes of care, assistance and supervision to an approved agency.

(3) *Homes and Hostels for the Blind.* "Home" means a residential institution for the care and maintenance of adult blind persons, who, owing to age or infirmity, are incapable of work, and are in

---

(a) See Appendix IV.
(b) *MacGillivray* v. *Northern Counties Institute for the Blind*
[1911] S.C. 897.

need of accommodation which cannot be provided otherwise than in an institution. "Hostel" means a residential institution for the provision of board and lodging for blind persons.

(4) *Home Teaching.* A Home Teacher is a person paid and employed by an approved agency to teach adult blind persons in their own homes how to read embossed type, to read to them, and to instruct them in simple forms of home occupations.

(5) *Book Production.*

(6) *Counties Associations,* which means the association of agencies operating in any group of counties for which a Local Advisory Committee has been constituted.

(7) *Miscellaneous Services,* having for their object the betterment of the conditions of the Blind or the prevention of blindness.

Considerable importance is attached to registration of the Blind, and it is considered desirable by the Ministry that the existing form of registration should be maintained.(*a*) The special registers of workshop employees, inmates of homes and hostels, and of the amount of work done by home workers required by Circular 7 B.D. of the Ministry of Health are also considered as desirable to be maintained.(*b*)

Powers and Duties of Local Authorities.

It is now necessary to consider the important powers conferred upon Local Authorities by the

(*a*) As to this, see p. 50, *post.*
(*b*) See Appendix IV.

Blind Persons Act, 1920 (c. 49), to promote the welfare of blind persons. It is the duty of the council of every county and county borough, whether in combination with any other council or councils or otherwise, to make arrangements to the satisfaction of the Minister of Health for promoting the welfare of blind persons ordinarily resident within their area.(a)   A blind person who becomes an inmate of an institution for the blind after September 19th, 1920, is deemed to continue to be ordinarily resident in the area in which he was ordinarily resident before he became an inmate of such institution.(b)

For the purpose of carrying out this duty the council may provide and maintain or contribute towards the provision and maintenance of workshops, hostels, homes, or other places for the reception of blind persons whether within or without their area and, with the approval of the Minister of Health, do such other things as may appear to them desirable.(c)   It has been decided by the Ministry of Health that the Blind Persons Act does not authorise the provision by a local authority of treatment or glasses which may prevent a seeing man from becoming blind.

Schemes by Local Authorities.

Councils were required, within twelve months after the passing of the Blind Persons Act, to prepare and

---

(a) Blind Persons Act, 1920 (c. 49), s. 2 (1).
(b) *Ibid.*, s. 2 (7).
(c) *Ibid.*, s. 2 (1).

submit to the Minister of Health a scheme for the exercise of their powers.(a)   With regard to these schemes, the Ministry of Health have addressed the following information to Local Authorities(b) :—

(1) Local Authorities may themselves make the necessary provision for the Blind, or may assist existing agencies.   In the latter case the council should be represented on the governing body of the agency.

(2) Local Authorities should, where necessary, formulate combined schemes, owing to the scattered distribution of blind persons.

(3) Schemes should include the following matters :—

(a) Children under school age, where the home conditions are unsatisfactory.

(b) Education and training of children and young persons and adults.(c)

(c) Employment of the Blind.(d)

(d) Home Workers.(e)

(e) Home Teaching.(f)

(f) Hostels and Homes.(g)

(g) Unemployable Blind.(h)

(h) Registration of the Blind.

(a) Blind Persons Act, 1920 (c. 49), s. 2 (1).
(b) Ministry of Health Circular 133 (1920).
(c) See Chapter 5, *post*.
(d) See Circular 7 B.D., and p. 46, *ante*.   As to sliding scale payments for workers in workshops, see Circular 64 B.D. (1922).
(e) See Circular 7 B.D., and p. 46, *ante*.
(f) See Circular 7 B.D., and p. 47, *ante*.
(g) See Circular 7 B.D. and p. 46, *ante*.
(h) See Chapter 4, *post*.

L. R. B.

Registration of the Blind.

The Register of the ·Blind forms an essential part
of the arrangements for the welfare of the Blind, and
is the subject of a Ministry of Health Circular.(a)
The Local Authority are liable for the compilation
and maintenance of records, by means of which the
central register is kept up to date. The actual work
of compilation may be delegated to the local voluntary agencies, and arrangements have to be made
whereby the records of blind persons moving from
the area of one Local Authority may be transferred
to that of another. No precise form is prescribed,
but it is considered advisable that they should be
kept in a form which will enable particulars to be
ascertained of the number of Blind in each district of
each sex and of the ages 0–5, 5–16, 16–21, 21–30, and
thereafter for each period of ten years up to 70 ; the
number under school age ; the number of children
of school age at school, and not at school ; the
number of blind persons under training ; the number
of blind persons in employment and occupations ;
the number in each category of deaf, mentally defective or physically defective blind, together with
the age incidence of blindness.

Suitable headings under which records should be
kept are set out in the Circular.(b)   The definition of
blindness adopted by the Ministry of Health must be
borne in mind.(c)

(a) Circular 64 B.D. (1922).
(b) *Ibid.*
(c) See p. 38, *ante.*

Certain difficulties arising from the registration of children are pointed out in a Ministry of Health Circular of 1932,(a) to which is scheduled extracts from a special report of the Advisory Committee on the Welfare of the Blind.   The Committee point out that as to blind children under school age there is some confusion between the Blind Persons Act Committee and the Child Welfare Committee, resulting in faulty registration ; they advise that the register should cover *all* blind persons whatever their age, and in case of doubt the child should be registered.   Again, as to children between 5 and 16, there are difficulties arising both from the educational definition of blindness being wider than that under the Blind Persons Act, and from a certain lack of liaison between the registration authority and the Local Education Authority.   It is suggested that for registration purposes children may be divided into those who are, or would be, taught by Braille, and those who are not.

Exercise of Powers through Committee.

Any of the powers of a council under the Blind Persons Act may be exercised through a committee of the council.   Persons specially qualified by training or experience in matters relating to the Blind who are not members of the council may be appointed to the committee, but not less than two-thirds of the members of the committee must be members of the council.   The committee may, subject to the direction

(a) Circular 162 B.D. (1932).

of the council, appoint sub-committees consisting either wholly or partly of members of the committee, as the committee thinks fit.(a)

Powers and Duties as to Blind Children.

The powers and duties of Local Authorities in relation to blind children under the Education Act, 1921 (c. 51), replacing the Elementary Education (Blind and Deaf Children) Act, 1893 (c. 42), are not affected, and in the exercise of their duty to contribute to the establishment of a national system of public education available for all persons capable of profiting thereby, Local Authorities are required to make or otherwise secure adequate and suitable provision for the technical education of blind persons ordinarily resident in their area who are capable of receiving and being benefited by such education.(b)

Exercise of Powers in London.

In the City of London these duties towards the Blind are to be carried out by the Common Council as if it were the council of a county borough.(c)

Expenses.

Provision is made for the expenses incurred in fulfilling these requirements. In the case of a county council they may be defrayed out of the county fund as expenses for general county purposes ; in the case

(a) Blind Persons Act, 1920 (c. 49), s. 2 (4).
(b) *Ibid.*, s. 2 (6).
(c) *Ibid.*, s. 2 (5).

of a county borough council out of the borough fund or borough rate ; (a) in the case of the Common Council of the City of London out of the general rate.(b) Further, a county council may borrow for the purpose of meeting these expenses, in accordance with the provisions relating to borrowing powers contained in sections 69 and 70 of the Local Government Act, 1888 (c. 41), while the council of a county borough may borrow in accordance with the Public Health Acts, 1875 to 1908. Money borrowed by the council of a county borough must be secured on the borough fund or borough rate.(c) It must be observed that the powers relating to raising rates or borrowing cannot be exercised through a committee of the council.(d)

Prevention of Blindness.

The activities of Local Authorities are not confined to promoting the welfare of the Blind. In addition, county councils and Local Authorities are empowered by the Public Health Act, 1925, to make such arrangements as they may think desirable to assist the prevention of blindness, subject to the consent of the Ministry of Health.(e) They may act through a committee of the council, which may include persons specially qualified by training or experience in matters relating to the Blind, who are not members

---

(a) Blind Persons Act, 1920 (c. 49), s. 2 (2).
(b) Ibid., s. 2 (5).
(c) Ibid., s. 2 (3).
(d) Ibid., s. 2 (4).
(e) Public Health Act, 1925 (c. 71), s. 66 (1).

of the council, but not less than two-thirds of the
members of the committee must be members of the
council. The committee may, subject to the direction of the council, appoint sub-committees consisting either wholly or partly of members of the
committee as the committee thinks fit.(a)

These powers include in particular the treatment
of persons ordinarily resident within the area of the
county council or Local Authority, who are suffering
from any disease of or injury to the eyes.(b) A
person who becomes an inmate of any hospital or
institution after September 7th, 1925, is deemed to
continue to be ordinarily resident in the area in which
he was ordinarily resident before he became an inmate of such hospital or institution.(c)

Expenses.

The expenses incurred in carrying out these powers
may be defrayed as expenses for general county purposes. If the Minister of Health by order so directs,
they may be defrayed as expenses for special county
purposes charged on such part of the county as may
be provided by the order.(d) A power of raising a
rate or of borrowing money in connection with the
prevention of blindness must be exercised by the
council and not by a committee of the council.(e)

(a) Public Health Act, 1925 (c. 71), s. 66 (3).
(b) Ibid., s. 66 (1).
(c) Ibid., s. 66 (4).
(d) Ibid., s. 66 (2).
(e) Ibid., s. 66 (3).

Publication of Information.

There is a general provision in the Public Health Act (a) by which a Local Authority or county council may arrange for the publication within their area of information on health and disease ; also for the delivery of lectures and the display of pictures in which such questions are dealt with.   This power may well be used as part of any suitable arrangements for the prevention or treatment of blindness under section 66 of the Act.

Infantile Ophthalmia.

Ophthalmia neonatorum was made notifiable in 1914, as an endemic and infectious disease.   This disease is defined as a purulent discharge from the eyes of an infant commencing within twenty-one days from the date of its birth.   The regulations relating to notification by the medical practitioner are now contained in S.R. & O. 1926, No. 971, as amended by S.R. & O. 1928, No. 419.

Blind Delinquents.

As to the position of blind delinquents, the Ministry of Health have informed local Voluntary Associations (b) that Chief Constables are being asked, whenever criminal proceedings are being taken against a blind person, to inform the appropriate county association, unless the blind person concerned objects.

(a) Public Health Act, 1925 (c. 71), s. 67.
(b) Ministry of Health Circular 162 B.D. (1932).

CHAPTER 4.

POOR LAW AND PENSIONS.

IT is the duty of the father, grandfather, mother, grandmother, husband or child, of a blind person not able to work, if possessed of sufficient means, to relieve and maintain that person.(a) Doubt has been expressed by the Advisory Committee on the Welfare of the Blind as to whether this provision applies to blind persons assisted under the Blind Persons Act, 1920 (c. 49).(b)

Duties of Local Authorities.

It is the duty of the council of every county and county borough to provide such relief as may be necessary for blind persons who are not able to work.(c) The council in preparing an administrative scheme under the Local Government Act, 1929 (c. 17), section 4, must have regard to the desirability of securing that all assistance which can lawfully be provided otherwise than by way of poor relief shall be so provided. Accordingly any such scheme may declare that any assistance which could

(a) Poor Law Act, 1930 (c. 17), s. 14.
(b) See Report of the Advisory Committee, July 17th, 1929.
(c) Poor Law Act, 1930 (c. 17), s 15 (1) (b).

be provided either by way of poor relief or by virtue
of the Blind Persons Act shall be provided exclusively by virtue of that Act and not by way of poor
relief.(a)　The duty of the council to provide poor
relief by the Poor Law Act, 1930 (c. 17), section 15,
is not in any way diminished.(b)　The Local Authorities had no power under the Blind Persons Act to
deal with the sighted dependants of the unemployable Blind.　But now, where a declaration is made
under section 5 (1) of the Local Government Act,
1929 (c. 17), this assistance may be given by a Public
Assistance Committee acting under section 6 (3) of
the Local Government Act, 1929 (c. 17).(c)

Meaning of Assistance.

Assistance includes maintenance and treatment at
hospitals and other places, the education of children
and any other services which could be provided
either by way of poor relief or by virtue of the Blind
Persons Act.(d)

Powers of Local Authorities.

The council of any county or county borough may
provide for the reception, maintenance, or instruction of any adult blind person in receipt of relief, in
any institution established for the reception of persons suffering from blindness.　They may also pay

---

(a) Local Government Act, 1929 (c. 17), s. 5, and as to assistance
under the Blind Persons Act, see Chapter 3, ante.
(b) Ibid., s. 5.
(c) See Report of the Advisory Committee, July 17th, 1929.
(d) Local Government Act, 1929 (c. 17), s. 5.

the charges incurred in the conveyance of any such blind person to and from the institution, as well as the expenses incurred in his maintenance, support and instruction in the institution.(a)

The councils of counties and county boroughs have power to subscribe to any institution for blind persons, or any institution for aiding such persons. The consent of the Minister of Health is necessary, and no subscription to an institution is authorised unless he is satisfied that persons receiving relief from the council have, or could have, assistance in such institution.(b)

Poor Blind Children.

As to children, the council of any county or county borough may send any poor blind child who is

(a) an idiot or imbecile ; or
(b) resident in a workhouse or in an institution to which he has been sent by a county or county borough council from a workhouse ; or
(c) boarded out by a county or county borough council,

to any school fitted for the reception of such children, whether or not the school is a certified school. The approval of the Ministry of Health is necessary. In no other circumstances may a blind child be sent to school in the exercise of poor law functions by a council.(c)

(a) Poor Law Act, 1930 (c. 17), s. 39.
(b) *Ibid.*, s. 67.
(c) *Ibid.*, s. 58; and see, also, pp. 92-96, *post.*

Removal.

One case on the removal of persons in receipt of relief is of importance to blind persons, and must be noted here. No order may be made by justices for the removal of any person becoming chargeable to a county or county borough in respect of relief made necessary by " sickness or accident " unless the justices making the order state therein that they are satisfied that the sickness or accident will produce permanent disability.(a) It has been held, construing a similar provision in an earlier Poor Law Act that " sickness " in this connection includes blindness.(b) In his judgment Lord Campbell, C.J., says :—

" It seems impossible to give any definition of " sickness which will not include blindness. A " disease which is incurable or mortal is none the " less sickness. Blindness may be incurable with- " out necessarily producing permanent disability " to earn a livelihood ; and a man though incurably " blind might be oppressively removed contrary to " the intentions of the statute."(c)

Effect of Relief under Blind Persons Act.

It is a disqualification from being, or becoming, a member of the council of a county or a county borough that a person who has within twelve months before becoming, or has since becoming, such a

(a) Poor Law Act, 1930 (c. 17), s. 95.
(b) R. v. Bucknell (Inhabitants) (1854) 3 E. & B. 587.
(c) Ibid., at p. 595.

member, received poor relief. The receipt of relief which could have been granted under the Blind Persons Act, however, is not alone sufficient to cause such disqualification.(a)

Pensions.

The right of a blind person to a pension at the age of fifty was given by the Blind Persons Act, 1920 (c. 49), section 1. Every blind person is entitled to receive such pension as he would be entitled to receive under the Old Age Pensions Acts, 1908-1919 on fulfilment of the following conditions :—

(a) He must have attained the age of fifty. The age of fifty is attained on the commencement of the day previous to the fiftieth anniversary.(b)

(b) He must be so blind as to be unable to perform work for which eyesight is essential.(c)

(c) If he is a natural born British subject he must since attaining the age of thirty have resided in the United Kingdom for an aggregate period of at least twelve years.

(d) In all other respects the provisions of the Old Age Pensions Acts, 1908–1919, apply, except section 10, sub-section 2 of the Old Age Pensions Act, 1908 (c. 40), requiring the giving of notices of death to pensions officers, by registrars of births and deaths. Notwithstanding this exception Rule 27 (1) (b) of the Old Age

(a) Local Government Act, 1929 (c. 17), s. 10 (1).
(b) Old Age Pensions Act, 1911 (c. 16), s. 1.
(c) As to this, see p. 39, ante.

Pensions Consolidated Regulations, 1922 (a) requires a return by registrars of births and deaths in respect of all deaths of blind persons under the age of seventy years who are stated to have been in receipt of old age pensions, which have been registered by him in the week immediately preceding the date of the return.

Evidence of Blindness.

In the investigation of a claim by a pensions officer regard may be had to the following for evidence as to blindness :(b)

(1) Certificate from the authorities of an approved school for the Blind that the claimant was educated as a blind person at the school.

(2) Certificate that the claimant was employed as a blind person at an approved workshop for the Blind.

(3) Certificate by the authorities of an approved agency for the Blind that the claimant is known to them as blind.

(4) Any other evidence which appears sufficient for the purpose.

Unemployment Insurance.

Blind persons in receipt of pensions are not required to pay contributions in respect of unemployment insurance.(c)

(a) S.R. & O. 1921, No. 2001.
(b) Ibid., Sched. II.
(c) Unemployment Insurance Act, 1920 (c. 30), s. 5 (5), as extended by Unemployment Insurance (No. 2) Act, 1924 (c. 30), s. 16, Sched. II,

CHAPTER 5.

THE EDUCATION OF THE BLIND.

LOCAL Education Authorities in the exercise of their duty to contribute to the establishment of a national system of public education available for all persons capable of profiting thereby are required to make or otherwise secure adequate and suitable provision for the technical education of blind persons ordinarily resident in their area who are capable of receiving and being benefited by such education.(a)   A person who becomes an inmate of an institution for the Blind after September 10th, 1920, is deemed to continue to be ordinarily resident in the area in which he was ordinarily resident before he became an inmate of such institution.(b)   For the purpose of carrying out this duty the council of every county and county borough may, and when required by the Board of Education, must submit to the Board of Education schemes showing how the duty is to be performed.(c)

The special statutory provisions relating to the compulsory education of blind children are to be found in the Education Act, 1921 (c. 51), Part V,

(a) Blind Persons Act, 1920 (c. 49), s. 2 (6).
(b) Ibid., s. 2 (7).
(c) Education Act, 1921 (c. 51), s. 11, and see generally Education Act, 1921 (c. 51), Part II.

which replaces with alterations, the Elementary
Education (Blind and Deaf Children) Act, 1893
(c. 42).

Who are Blind Children.

A child is blind for the purpose of these provisions
who is too blind to be able to read the ordinary school
books used by children.(a)   The period of compulsory
education is from the age of five years, or six years if
so provided by a by-law under the Education Act,(b)
until the age of sixteen :(c) a child who attains the
age of sixteen during the school term is not deemed
to have reached that age until the end of the term.(d)

Duty of Parent.

The duty of a parent to cause his child to receive
efficient elementary education in reading, writing,
and arithmetic (e) extends, in the case of a blind
child, to instruction suitable to such a child.(f)
It is to be observed that elementary education may
include industrial training.(g)   The fact that a child
is blind, or the fact that there is not within any
particular distance from the residence of a blind
child any public elementary school which the child
can attend is not of itself a reasonable excuse for

(a) Education Act, 1921 (c. 51), s. 69.
(b) Ibid., s. 42.
(c) Ibid., s. 61.
(d) Ibid., s. 138 (1).
(e) Ibid., s. 42.
(f) Ibid., s. 51 (1).
(g) Ibid., s. 69.

not causing the child to attend school, or for neglect-
ing to provide efficient elementary instruction for the
child.(a)   There is a general provision in the Education Act that distance from school is not a reasonable
excuse for non-attendance, when suitable means of
conveyance for a child between a reasonable distance
of its home and a public elementary school is provided,(b) and Local Authorities are empowered to
provide guides or conveyances for children who by
reason of any physical or mental defect are unable
to attend school without such guides or conveyances.(c)   Where such a conveyance is provided
failure to provide also an attendant to help the children in and out constitutes negligence for which the
Local Authority are liable in damages.(d)

Standard of Diligence of Local Authority.

The standard of diligence of a Local Authority
towards blind children is that which would be observed by a reasonable parent.   In a Scottish case (e)
a blind boy aged seven, an inmate of a hostel provided by an education authority, was injured
through being knocked down by a boy who unex-
pectedly jumped on his back while he was at play in
a room with other children, some of whom were not
blind.   The accident occurred when there was no
one in charge of the children, and it was alleged that

(a) Education Act, 1921 (c. 51), s. 51 (2).
(b) Ibid., s. 49.
(c) Ibid., s. 88 (2).
(d) Shrimpton v. Hertfordshire County Council (1911) 104 L.T.
145.
(e) Gow v. Glasgow Education Authority [1922] S.C. 260.

the accident was due to negligence, since there was a duty to provide constant supervision, especially when the children were allowed to play with sighted children. It was held, however, that there was no duty to provide constant supervision, and that the accident could not have been prevented had a supervisor been present. In the course of the judgment Lord Sands said :(a)

> "The case would have presented a different "aspect if the accident had been one which might "have been foreseen as not wholly unlikely to occur "—if, for example, blind boys had been left to romp "by themselves in a room where there was an un-"guarded fire and one of them had run into it and "been burned. . . . I do not think any higher "standard of precaution is incumbent upon the "defenders than would be observed by a reasonable "parent."

Duty of Local Authority.

It is the duty of the Local Authority for elementary education to enable blind children resident in their area, for whose elementary education (which may include industrial training),(b) provision is not otherwise made, to obtain that education in some school for the time being certified by the Board of Education as suitable for providing that education.(c) "School" includes any institution in which blind

---

(a) *Gow* v. *Glasgow Education Authority* [1922] S.C. 260, at p. 267.
(b) Education Act, 1921 (c. 51), s. 69.
(c) *Ibid.*, s. 52 (1).

L. R. B.

F

children are boarded or lodged as well as taught, and any establishment for boarding or lodging children taught in a school certified as a school for blind children.(*a*)

Area in which Children Resident.

As regards the expression " resident in their area " a child resident in a school or boarded out in pursuance of the Education Act is deemed to be resident in the area from which the child is sent.(*b*) The duty of the authority does not extend to idiots or imbeciles ;(*c*) with regard to children resident in a workhouse or in any institution to which they have been sent by a board of guardians (*d*) from a workhouse, or boarded out by guardians,(*d*) see the Education (Institution Children) Act, 1923, dealt with on p. 91 *post.*

Discharge of Duty of Local Authority.

The duty of the Local Authority outlined above may be discharged in three ways :

(1) They may establish or acquire and maintain a certified school,(*e*) in which case, they have the same powers in relation to the provisions of Special

(*a*) Education Act, 1921 (c. 51), s. 69.
(*b*) *Ibid.*, s. 52 (4).
(*c*) *Ibid.*, s. 52 (2).
(*d*) See now Local Government Act, 1929 (c. 17), s. 1, by which guardians are abolished and their functions transferred to the councils of counties and county boroughs.
(*e*) Education Act, 1921 (c. 51), s. 52 (1).

Schools as they have in relation to the provision of school accommodation under Part III of the Education Act.(a) Schools for blind children provided by the Local Education Authority for the administrative county of London are not to be treated as public elementary schools for the purpose of the rules relating to the management of provided schools in London.(b)

(2) They may contribute on such terms and to such extent as may be approved by the Board of Education towards the establishment or enlargement, alteration, and maintenance of a school so certified, or towards any of these purposes.(c) In this case the terms approved by the Board of Education must, where the school is maintained by another authority, include security for repayment of the value of the contribution in the event of the school ceasing to be certified, and may, where it appears to the Board to be practicable or expedient, include provision for representation of the contributing Education Authority on the governing body of the school.(d)

(3) They may, when necessary or expedient, make arrangements, subject to regulations of the Board, for boarding out any blind child in a home conveniently near to the certified school where the child is receiving elementary education.(e)

(a) Education Act, 1921 (c. 51), s. 62.
(b) Ibid., s. 36 (4).
(c) Ibid., s. 52 (1).
(d) Ibid., s. 52 (3).
(e) Ibid., s. 52 (1).

Boarding-out Regulations.

Regulations relating to boarding-out are contained in S.R. & O. 1909, No. 860, as amended by S.R. & O. 1917, No. 591, and are as follows :—

(1) A Local Education Authority may, subject to the provisions of these regulations, board out blind or deaf children resident in their district in homes conveniently near to a school for the time being certified by the Board of Education as suitable for providing elementary education for such children respectively, under arrangements approved by the Board of Education with a Boarding-out Committee, constituted as hereinafter mentioned.

(2) A Boarding-out Committee shall consist of three or more persons, to be approved by the Board of Education, who shall have signed an engagement in the Form annexed to this Order.(a)

(3) Any person deriving any pecuniary or other personal profit from the boarding-out of any child shall be thereby disqualified from becoming or continuing to be a member of any such Boarding-out Committee.

(4) The Boarding-out Committee shall from time to time appoint one of their members to act as Secretary ; and it shall be the duty of the Secretary punctually to inform the Board of Education of any vacancies which may be caused by

(a) See S.R. & O. 1909, No. 860, Sched. I.

death, resignation, or otherwise, amongst the members of the Committee, and to submit the names of the persons proposed to fill the vacancies.

(5) A child may be withdrawn from a home by its parent or by the Local Education Authority of the district from which the child is sent, notice of the intention to do so being given at least one week beforehand to the Boarding-out Committee ; and the foster-parent shall, upon the demand of a person duly authorised in writing by the Boarding-out Committee, or by the Local Education Authority, or by the parent, deliver up the child to such person.

(6) The Regulations to be observed by the Local Education Authority with respect to such Boarding-out of blind or deaf children shall be as follows :—

(1) There shall not be more than two blind or deaf children boarded-out in the same home at the same time.

(2) No blind child shall be boarded out in a home where there is a deaf child, nor a deaf child where there is a blind child.

(3) No child shall be boarded-out in a home in which at the time when the child would first be placed in it, there would be with such child more than four children resident, or in which any pauper child is boarded-out by the guardians. (a)

(4) No child shall be boarded-out with any person who is at the time, or who has been within

(a) See note (d), p. 66, ante.

12 months preceding, in receipt of relief ; and if the foster-parent shall at any time become in receipt of relief any child boarded-out with him shall be withdrawn from him.

(5) The Local Education Authority shall, if possible, arrange for the boarding-out being with a person belonging to the religious persuasion of the child's parent.

(6) No child shall be boarded-out without a certificate, in the Form annexed to this Order,(a) signed by a duly qualified medical practitioner, stating the particulars of the child's health, such certificate to be forwarded by the Local Education Authority to the Boarding-out Committee.

(7) Before receiving any child to be boarded-out with him, the foster-parent shall sign an undertaking in duplicate, which shall, in addition to any other matter which may be agreed upon, contain an engagement on the part of the foster-parent, that in consideration of a certain sum per week, he will bring up the child as one of his own children, and provide the child with proper food, lodging, and washing, and endeavour to train the child in habits of truthfulness, obedience, personal cleanliness, and industry, as well as in such special industry or occupations as may be prescribed by the managers of the certified school which the child attends ; that he will take care that the child shall attend duly at church or chapel

(a) See S.R. & O. 1909, No. 860, Sched. II.

according to the religious denomination to which the child belongs, and shall attend the particular certified school directed by the Local Education Authority according to the provisions of the law for the time being, and will make such provision as may be necessary for the escort of the child to and from church or chapel and school ; that he will provide for the proper repair and renewal of the child's clothing, and that, in case of the child's illness, he will forthwith report such illness to the Local Education Authority, to the child's parent, and to the Boarding-out Committee ; and that he will at all reasonable times permit the child to be visited by his parent, and will at all times permit the child to be visited, and the house to be inspected by any member of the Boarding-out Committee, and by any person specially appointed for that purpose by the Local Education Authority or by the Board of Education. The undertaking shall also contain an engagement on the part of the foster-parent that he will, upon the demand of the child's parent or of a person duly authorised in writing by him or by the Boarding-out Committee, or by the Local Education Authority, give up possession of the child.

Such undertaking shall be made in triplicate according to the Form annexed to this Order.(a) One copy of it shall be kept by the foster-parent, another by the Local

(a) See S.R. & O. 1909, No. 860, Sched. III.

Education Authority, and another by the child's parent.

(8) On the delivery of the child to the foster-parent an acknowledgment shall be given in the Form hereinafter prescribed,(a) or to the like effect.

(9) In no case shall the sum to be paid to the foster-parent for the maintenance of a child, inclusive of lodging, but exclusive of clothing, school-fees, fees for medical attendance, medicines, and extras ordered by a medical attendant, be less than six or (except with the consent of the Board of Education) (b) more than ten shillings per week.

(10) Unless arrangements can be made for transit by some public conveyance, no child shall be boarded-out in a home more than one mile from the certified school which the child attends.

(11) The managers of the certified school shall undertake to receive the child and to send to the Local Education Authority at least once a quarter a written report upon the child, in the Form annexed to this Order.(c)

(12) No child shall be boarded-out in any home which is distant more than five miles by the nearest road of access from the residence of some member of the Boarding-out Committee.

(7) Every boarded-out child shall be visited not

(a) See S.R. & O. 1909, No. 860, Sched. IV.
(b) The words in brackets were added by S.R. & O. 1917, No. 591.
(c) See S.R. & O. 1909, No. 860, Sched. V.

less often than once in every month by a member
or officer of the Boarding-out Committee at the
home of the foster-parent and the visitor shall
thereupon make a report in writing to the Committee, mentioning the apparent bodily condition
and the behaviour of such child, and the state of
the home and all reasonable complaints made by
the child or the foster-parent.

These reports shall be forwarded by the Boarding-out Committee to the Local Education Authority and to the child's parent not less often than
quarterly.

If in the case of any boarded-out child no such
report shall be received by the Local Education
Authority or the parent for the space of four
consecutive months, the Local Education Authority shall in default of satisfactory explanation
withdraw the child from the home with all reasonable expedition.

(8) (1) The Local Education Authority shall, as
soon as practicable after the first day of April and
the first day of October in every year, make a
return to the Board of Education, in the Form
annexed to this Order,(a) of the several children
remaining so boarded-out on those dates respectively. Separate returns shall be made for blind
and deaf children respectively.

(2) The Secretary to the Boarding-out Committee shall make a return to the Board of Education as soon as practicable after the first day of
January and the first day of July in every year of

_____

(a) See S.R. & O. 1909, No. 860, Sched. VI.

the several children remaining boarded-out under the supervision of the Committee on those days respectively under these Regulations. Such return shall be made according to the prescribed Form,(*a*) and shall be made separately for blind and deaf children respectively.

(9) If the Board of Education shall withdraw from any Boarding-out Committee the authority to enter into arrangements with Local Education Authorities, the Local Education Authorities who have made arrangements with the said Committee for the boarding-out of children shall, on receiving notice of such withdrawal, provide with all reasonable expedition for the return of all children boarded out in homes found by such Committee to their own homes or for their transfer to homes found by another Boarding-out Committee. Provided that it shall not be necessary for the Local Education Authority to take back such children if the Board of Education declare that the withdrawal of authority from the Committee shall not apply to children already boarded-out under their superintendence.

(10) Where the arrangements made by a Local Education Authority with any Boarding-out Committee under these Regulations include the payment of any sums by such Committee on behalf of the Local Education Authority, the Local Education Authority may, if they think fit, advance to the Boarding-out Committee quarterly ·a sum not exceeding three-fourths of the expendi-

---

(*a*) See S.R. & O. 1909, No. 860, Sched. VII.

ture, which in pursuance of such arrangements, may reasonably be expected to be incurred by such Committee during the ensuing quarter.

(11) In this Order :—

The term " foster-parent " means the persons or person with whom any child is boarded-out under the provisions of this Order.

Other expressions have, unless the contrary intention appears, the same meaning as in the Elementary Education (Blind and Deaf Children) Act, 1893.(a)

All words importing the masculine gender shall be deemed and taken to include females, and the singular to include the plural, and the plural the singular, unless the contrary as to gender or number is expressly provided.

Certified Schools.

Reference has been made to certified schools : the requirements of the Education Act in regard to certification are these : A school must not be certified by the Board of Education as suitable for providing elementary education for blind children unless the following requirements are complied with :—

(a) It must not be conducted for private profit ;(b)
(b) It must be managed by a Local Education Authority, or the annual expenses of its maintenance must be audited and published in

(a) Now repealed and replaced by the Education Act, 1921 (c. 51).

(b) Education Act, 1921 (c. 51), s. 63 (1) (a).

accordance with Regulations of the Board of
Education ;(*a*)

(c) It must be open at all times to the inspection of
His Majesty's Inspectors of schools and of any
visitors authorised by any local education
authority sending children to the school ;(*b*)

(d) The requirements of Part V of the Education
Act must be complied with in the case of the
school.(*c*)

The certificate is an annual one (*d*) and once certified
a school may be treated as a public elementary school
for the purpose of school attendance orders in respect
of children to whom Part V of the Education Act
applies.(*e*)

Regulations as to Certified Schools.

Certified schools and classes providing elementary
education for blind children are referred to in the
Board of Education (Special Services) Regulations,
1925,(*f*) as Special Schools, and the following regulations apply :—

(1) Special Schools may be certified as day
schools ; or as boarding schools in which
children are boarded, lodged and taught ; or as
homes in which children taught in Special
Schools are boarded and lodged.(*g*)

(*a*) Education Act, 1921 (c. 51), s. 63 (1) (b), and see p. 81, *post*.
(*b*) *Ibid.*, s. 63 (1) (c).
(*c*) *Ibid.*, s. 63 (1) (d).
(*d*) *Ibid.*, s. 63 (3).
(*e*) *Ibid.*, s. 63 (2).
(*f*) S.R. & O. 1925, No. 835. (Grant Regulations, No. 19.)
(*g*) *Ibid.*, r. 24 (2).

(2) No child may be admitted to or retained in a Special School if he does not belong to the type of child for which the school is designed, or if he cannot be instructed in the school without detriment to the interest of the other children.(*a*)

(3) No child may be admitted to a Special School under two years of age, and no child may be retained in a Special School after the end of the term in which he completes sixteen years of age.(*b*)

(4) Boys and girls attending a boarding school or home must be separated for all purposes other than meals, lessons and recreation under supervision, except under circumstances approved by the Board.(*c*)

(5) The curriculum and time-table of the school must be approved by the Board.(*d*)

(6) The school must meet not less than 400 times in each year commencing 1st April, subject to a proportionate reduction for periods of less than a year.(*e*)

(7) In calculating the number of times on which the school has met, an allowance of nine meetings may be made for each week during which the school has been closed on medical authority or for any other unavoidable cause.(*f*)

(*a*) S.R. & O. 1925, No. 835, r. 24 (3).
(*b*) *Ibid.*, r. 24 (4).
(*c*) *Ibid.*, r. 24 (5).
(*d*) *Ibid.*, r. 25.
(*e*) *Ibid.*, r. 26 (1).
(*f*) *Ibid.*, r. 26 (2).

(8) Unless the Board otherwise determine, a meeting must not exceed two and a half hours and must provide for at least two hours of secular instruction including recreation and games, but excluding registration.(a)

(9) The rules as to school records and the registration of attendances at Public Elementary Schools must, so far as applicable, be observed, provided that where the Medical Officer of the school considers on medical grounds that it would be detrimental to a child to remain under instruction during the whole meeting an attendance by such child of not less than one and a half hours at each meeting may be counted.(b)

(10) A Special School must be visited from time to time during school hours by the Managers or persons authorised by the Authority.(c)

(11) Blind, deaf and defective children attending Special Schools may be boarded out in accordance with the Regulations of the Board.(d)

(12) Before admission to a Special School a child must be certified to belong to the type of child for which the school is designed by a medical practitioner.(e)

(13) The medical practitioner shall, if so directed by the Authority, or if so requested by the parent of the child, before giving a certificate, consult the head teacher of the school (if any) which the

---

(a) S.R. & O. 1925, No. 835, r. 26 (3).
(b) Ibid., r. 26 (4).
(c) Ibid., r. 27.
(d) Ibid., r. 28, and see p. 68, ante.
(e) Ibid., r. 29 (1).

child has been attending, or such other person as the Authority may appoint for the purpose, and a copy of any report made by the head teacher or such other person shall be given to the Authority.(*a*)

(14) Adequate provision must be made for the medical inspection, supervision and treatment of the children by a medical practitioner possessing special experience of the particular defect from which the children suffer.(*b*)

(15) Students from a Training College must on request from the authorities of the College or from the Board be allowed to attend the school for the purpose of receiving practical instruction in teaching or for observation on such conditions as may be approved by the Board.(*c*)

Special Service Regulations.

In addition, the following general conditions apply to all institutions giving Special Services whether elementary education, or higher education :—

(1) The Authority must appoint a School Medical Officer, and such other medical officers, nurses and other persons as are necessary for the efficient discharge of their functions. The name of any person whose appointment as School Medical Officer is proposed must be submitted to the Board for approval before his appointment.(*d*)

(*a*) S.R & O. 1925, No. 835, r. 2. r. 29 (2).
(*b*) Ibid., r. 29 (3).
(*c*) Ibid., r. 30.
(*d*) Ibid., r. 2.

(2) The Authority's arrangements for the discharge of their functions relating to Special Services should be suitable to local needs and circumstances and should be properly related to the other services of education and public health in the area. Due regard must be had to the claims of each Special Service so that the Authority's provision as a whole may form a comprehensive and well-balanced scheme for promoting the physical and mental development of all the children in the area.(a)

(3) The Authority, if required by the Board, shall submit to the Board annually a statement showing their proposals in regard to Special Services for the 12 months beginning on the 1st April.(b)

(4) The Authority shall submit in respect of each calendar year a report from their School Medical Officer describing and tabulating the work of himself and his staff in respect of Special Services.(c)

(5) Any premises used for the purpose of a Special Service must be open at all times to inspection by an officer authorised by the Board.(d)

(6) Such records must be kept and returns furnished as the Board may from time to time require.(e)

(7) Any institution for the provision of Special

(a) S.R. & O. 1925, No. 835, r. 3 (1).
(b) *Ibid.*, r. 3 (2).
(c) *Ibid.*, r. 3 (3).
(d) *Ibid.*, r. 4.
(e) *Ibid.*, r. 5.

Services which is not provided by the Authority must comply with the following conditions :

(a) It must be under the direction of a body of Managers, who must appoint some person to act as Correspondent on their behalf with the Board.

(b) It must be suitable in character and financial position to receive aid from the Board and must not be conducted for private profit or farmed out by any member of the staff.

(c) Its accounts must be audited by a Member of the Institute of Chartered Accountants or of the Society of Incorporated Accountants and Auditors or by a Banker or Bank Manager, or, in cases where no person so qualified is available, by some person specially approved by the Board. Copies of the accounts must be forwarded to the Board.

(d) In the case of Special Schools copies of the accounts must be forwarded to all Authorities and other bodies by whom Children are sent to the school, and must be supplied to all persons applying for them, either gratuitously or at a charge not exceeding one penny. Public notice must be given that the accounts are open to inspection within reasonable hours.

(e) In the case of Special Schools and Courses of Higher Education an annual report must be furnished to the Board on the working of the institution including particulars as to the admission, retention, departure and after careers of pupils, the arrangements for attending to their health and any alterations to the premises.(a)

(8) Any premises used for the purpose of a Special Service must be suitably situated, healthy, safe in case of fire, adequately lighted, warmed, ventilated, cleaned and drained and adequately equipped and generally suitable for the purposes for which they are required.(b)

(9) Any proposal for acquiring a site or providing new premises or substantially enlarging or altering existing premises or involving substantial expenditure on equipment for the purpose of a Special Service must be submitted with an estimate of the cost and full particulars for the approval of the Board before any expenditure is incurred.(c)

(10) The teaching and other staff employed on Special Services must be sufficient and suitable and must be such as the Board may from time to time require.(d)

(11) Notice must be given to the Board, as and when required, of any change in the staff.(e)

(12) If a teacher is convicted of a criminal offence or his engagement is terminated, whether by way of dismissal or resignation, on account of

---

(a) S.R. & O. 1925, r. 6.
(b) *Ibid.*, r. 7.
(c) *Ibid.*, r. 8.
(d) *Ibid.*, r. 9 (1).
(e) *Ibid.*, r. 9 (2).

misconduct or grave professional default, the facts must at once be reported to the Board of Education.(*a*)

(13) The Board may refuse to recognise a teacher or other member of the staff temporarily or permanently and either generally or for particular purposes, and they may cancel or suspend any certificate or other evidence of qualifications issued by them. Before taking action the Board will use every available means of informing the person concerned of the grounds of their proposed action and of giving him an opportunity of making representations on the subject.(*b*)

(14) Teachers (other than occasional teachers) must be employed under written agreements or, in the case of schools provided by a Local Education Authority, under a minute of the Authority.(*c*)

(15) The agreement or minute must, either directly or by reference to specified regulations or minutes, define the conditions of service and indicate whether it is intended that the teacher shall be employed either :

(a) in full-time service and exclusively in the capacity of a teacher ; or

(b) in part-time service in the capacity of a teacher ; or

(c) partly in the capacity of a teacher and partly in another capacity.(*d*)

(*a*) S. R. & O. 1925, No. 835, r. 9 (3).
(*b*) Ibid., r. 9 (4).
(*c*) Ibid., r. 10 (1).
(*d*) Ibid., r. 10 (2).

(16) In the case of teachers in Special Schools the agreement or minute must include either expressly or by reference the following clause :

"The teacher shall not be required to perform any duties except such as are connected with the work of the school or institution or to abstain outside the hours of official duty from any occupations which do not interfere with the due performance of his duties as a teacher of the school or institution." (a)

(17) Any fees or other charges made in connection with a Special Service must be submitted for approval by the Board of Education if the Board so require.(b)

(18) The accommodation of any premises as assessed by the Board must not be exceeded.(c)

(19) If the Sanitary Authority of the district, or any two members of that Authority acting on the advice of the Medical Officer of Health, requires either the closure of any premises used for the purpose of a Special Service or the exclusion of certain pupils therefrom for a specified time with a view to preventing the spread of disease or any danger to health, the requirement must be at once complied with.(d)

(20) At least a full week's notice must be given to the Board's Inspector of the closure of any school or of any alteration in the time when it is

---

(a) S.R. & O. 1925, No. 835, r. 10 (3).
(b) *Ibid.*, r. 11.
(c) *Ibid.*, r. 12.
(d) *Ibid.*, r. 13.

usually opened, and if such notice cannot be given, notice must be given by telegram.(a)

(21) Any institution for the provision of Special Services must comply with the provisions of any Act of Parliament applicable thereto.(b)

(22) Where a child leaves a school provided or maintained by an Authority and enters another school not provided or maintained by that Authority, the Authority shall, if required by the Authority or Governors responsible for the school which he has entered, furnish them with particulars of the child's medical record.(c)

Report to Parliament.

The Board of Education in their annual report to Parliament are required to furnish particulars of their proceedings under Part V of the Education Act, and to give lists of the schools and classes to which they have granted or refused certificates during the year to which the report relates, with their reasons for such refusal.(d)

Enforcement of Attendance.

The attendance of a blind child at school may be enforced as if it were required by by-laws under Part IV of the Education Act.(e)

(a) S.R. & O. 1925, No. 835, r. 14.
(b) *Ibid.*, r. 15.
(c) *Ibid.*, r. 16.
(d) Education Act, 1921 (c. 51), s. 68.
(e) *Ibid.*, s. 61, and see s. 46 for the duty of the Local Education Authority to make by-laws.

Religious Education

As regards the religious education of a blind child, a child must not be compelled to receive religious instruction contrary to the wishes of the parent, and it must, so far as practicable, have facilities for receiving religious instruction and attending religious services conducted in accordance with the parent's persuasion, which must be duly registered on the child's admission to the school.(a)   In case of difference in religious persuasion the father's is preferred to the mother's, unless the parents are living apart, when that of the parent having lawful custody of the blind child will be the religious persuasion to be registered.

Payments under Part V of the Education Act are not to be made conditional on attendance at any school other than such as may be reasonably selected by the parent, nor refused because the child attends or does not attend any particular certified school.(b)

If the school which the child is attending is a public elementary school the provisions of section 27 of the Education Act must be complied with, in the matter of religious instruction.   If the school is not a public elementary school, it must, in all matters relating to the religious instruction and observances of the child, be conducted in accordance with the rules applying to industrial schools, and any local education authority may provide and maintain a school so

(a) Education Act, 1921 (c. 51), s. 64 (4).
(b) Ibid., s. 66.

conducted.(*a*)   In the provisions of the Children Act, 1908 (c. 67) (*b*) relating to industrial schools, and the rules made thereunder, references to the Secretary of State are to be construed as references to the Board of Education,(*c*) and every rule made must forthwith be laid before both Houses of Parliament.(*d*)

In selecting a school for a blind child the Local Education Authority must be guided by the rules relating to industrial schools, laid down by the Children Act, 1908 (c. 67), in regard to religious instruction.(*e*)

Where a child is boarded out under Part V of the Education Act the local education must, if possible, arrange for the boarding-out to be with a person belonging to the religious persuasion of the child's parent.(*f*)

Expenses of Blind Child.

The parent of a blind child may be liable for the expenses of the child.   Where the Local Education Authority incur any expense in respect of a blind child the parent of the child is liable to contribute towards the expenses of the child such weekly sum as may be agreed upon between the authority and the parent, regard being had to the duty of the Local

---

(*a*) Education Act, 1921 (c. 51), s. 64 (1).
(*b*) See note (*e*), *infra.*
(*c*) Education Act, 1921 (c. 51), s. 64 (1).
(*d*) *Ibid.*, s. 64 (2), and see Rules Publication Act, 1893 (c. 66).
(*e*) *Ibid.*, s. 64 (3), and see Children Act, 1908 (c. 67), s. 66, now repealed and replaced by the Children and Young Persons Act, 1932 (c. 46), s. 28 (4), Sched. I, 12, 26.
(*f*) Education Act, 1921 (c. 51), s. 64 (3), and compare p. 70, *ante.*

Education Authority to provide a sufficient amount of public school accommodation without payment of fees. If the parties fail to agree either party may apply to have the sum settled by a court of summary jurisdiction. The sum agreed on or settled by the court may be recovered by the Local Education Authority summarily as a civil debt, without pre-judiee to any other remedy.(a)

It is the duty of the Local Education Authority to enforce any order made under this section; (b) the order may be revoked or varied at any time by a court competent to make the order.(c)

Any sum received by the authority in respect of expenses may be applied in aid of their general expenses.(d)

Meaning of Expenses.

The expression " expenses " includes the expenses of and incidental to the attendance of a child at a school, and of, and incidental to, the maintenance and boarding-out of the child while so attending, and the expenses of conveying the child to and from the school.(e)

Meaning of Parent.

Parent includes a guardian and every person who is liable to maintain or has the actual custody of a

---

(a) Education Act, 1921 (c. 51), s. 65 (1).
(b) *Ibid.*, s. 65 (2).
(c) *Ibid.*, s. 65 (3).
(d) *Ibid.*, s. 65 (2).
(e) *Ibid.*, s. 69.

child.(*a*)   Where a child was left without any means of support, and without any relation legally liable to maintain him, the fact that the guardians of the union would be bound to support him if he became chargeable has been held not to make them " liable to maintain " him within this section. They were therefore not liable to contribute towards the expenses of boarding-out as being the " parent " of the child.(*b*)

Grants to Certified Schools.

The Board of Education are entitled to give aid from the Parliamentary Grant to a certified school in respect of education given to blind children to such amount and on such conditions as may be directed by or in pursuance of the regulations of the Board in force for the time being.(*c*)

These Grants, when paid in respect of such of the Special Services as are services of elementary education, are paid as part of the consolidated grant for elementary education under Grant Regulations No. 1.(*d*)

Grants to Non-provided Institutions.

Grants are also payable to institutions not provided by the Local Education Authority. These are payable for each year, commencing 1st April after

(*a*) Education Act, 1921 (c. 51), s. 170 (12).
(*b*) *Southwark Union* v. *London County Council* [1910] 2 K.B. 559.
(*c*) Education Act, 1921 (c. 51), s. 67.
(*d*) S.R. & O. 1925, No. 835, r. 1 (2).

the end of the year,(a) and they may be withheld or reduced if the conditions in the Board of Education (Special Services) Regulations, 1925,(b) are not fulfilled.(c)

Payment of grant to a school or institution which ceases to be recognised may be limited so as not to exceed the net outstanding liabilities for maintenance at the date from which recognition ceases.(d)

Calculation of Grant.

For the purpose of the calculation of grant based on average attendance :—

  (a) the average attendance for a year is the quotient of the total number of recognised attendances made during that year divided by the number of meetings, a fraction of a unit being ignored or reckoned as an additional unit according as it is or is not less than one half.

  (b) The Board will not recognise attendances made by a pupil on account of whom :

    (i) a payment is made by any local authority, or

    (ii) grant is payable by a Government Department other than the Board.

An exception will be allowed as regards attendances made before April 1st, 1931, by a pupil

---

(a) S.R. & O. 1925, No. 835, r. 39 (1) ; S.R. & O. 1931, No. 184, r. 2.
(b) S.R. & O. 1925, No. 835.
(c) Ibid., r. 43.
(d) Ibid., r. 39 (2) ; S.R. & O. 1931, No. 184, r. 2.

on account of whom a payment is made by a local authority under the Poor Law Act, 1930 (c. 17).

(c) The average attendance of day pupils and boarders will be reckoned separately.

(d) If the period for which the grant is payable is less than a year, the amount will be reduced proportionately.(a)

Amount of Grant.

The grant payable to a Special School for blind children comprises :—

(a) a sum in respect of each unit of average attendance, amounting to £7 10s. for a day pupil, and £15 10s. for a boarder

(b) a sum representing two and a half per cent. of the amount of the salaries paid in respect of employment in the school to teachers in contributory service, as calculated for the purposes of the Teachers (Superannuation) Act, 1925 (c. 59).(b)

Education of Children from other Areas.

The expenses of educating blind children in an area other than that to which they belong are now dealt with by the Education (Institution Children) Act, 1923 (c. 38), which must now be considered.

(a) S.R. & O. 1925, No. 835, r. 39 (3) ; S.R. & O. 1931, No. 184, r. 2.

(b) S.R. & O. 1925, No. 835, r. 40 (1) ; S.R. & O. 1931, No. 184, r. 2 ; S.R. & O., 1932, No. 19, r. 2.

Day Scholars.

As to day scholars, where in England or Wales children who are resident in a workhouse or in an institution to which they have been sent by a board of guardians from a workhouse or boarded out by the guardians,(a) or resident in a charitable institution, attend as day scholars a public elementary school or a school certified by the Board of Education under Part V of the Education Act, 1921, maintained by a Local Education Authority for elementary education of an area other than the area to which the children belong, the Local Education Authority of the area to which the children belong must, if required so to do by the Local Education Authority of the area in which the children are educated, pay to that authority in respect of each such child during the period of attendance, in the case of a child attending a certified school, a sum calculated by reference to the average net cost, falling to be met from the rates, in the last preceding financial year of educating children in schools in the last-mentioned area of the same type as the school which the child attends.(b)

Area to which Child Belongs.

A child who is resident in a workhouse or in an institution to which he has been sent by the guardians

---

(a) The guardians of the poor were abolished by the Local Government Act, 1929 (c. 17), s. 1, and their functions transferred to the councils of counties and county boroughs.

(b) Education (Institution Children) Act, 1923 (c. 38), s. 1 (1).

from a workhouse or boarded out by the guardians shall be deemed to belong to the area in which his place of settlement is situated, and a child resident in a charitable institution shall be deemed to belong :

(1) to the area in England and Wales in which he last resided for a continuous period of six months otherwise than in a charitable institution ; or

(2) if it cannot be ascertained that he has so resided in any area for six months, the area, being an area in England and Wales, in which he was born ; or

(3) if the Board of Education are of opinion that the area to which he belongs cannot be ascertained under (1) and (2), such area as the Board of Education may determine having regard to all the circumstances of the case.(a)

The guardians or the managers of the charitable institution as the case may be, must furnish to the Local Education Authority of the area in which the children are educated such information as may be necessary in order to enable that authority to determine to what area children educated in schools certified under Part V of the Education Act, belong.(b)

Meaning of Charitable Institution.

A charitable institution includes any place in which persons are boarded and lodged from motives

(a) Education (Institution Children) Act, 1923 (c. 38), s. 1 (2).
(b) Education (Institution Children) Act, 1923 (c. 38), s. 1 (3).

of charity, but does not include any place in which less than twelve children between the ages of five and fourteen are so boarded and lodged.(*a*)

Decision of Board of Education Final.

If any question arises as to the amount payable, or as to the area to which a child resident in a charitable institution belongs, or as to whether a child is resident in a charitable institution within the meaning of the section, the question must be referred to the Board of Education and the decision of the Board is final.(*b*)

Recovery of Expenses.

Any sum payable is recoverable as a debt due to the authority to whom it is payable, and the Board of Education may, if they think fit, without prejudice to any other remedy on the part of that authority, pay any such sum to the authority to whom it is payable and deduct any sums so paid from any sums payable to the authority by whom it is payable on account of Parliamentary Grants.(*c*)

No sum is payable unless a claim for payment is made within two years after the end of the financial year during which the attendances on which the claim is based were made.(*d*)

Contribution orders may be made by the Board of Education.(*e*)

(*a*) Education (Institution Children) Act, 1923 (c. 38), s. 1 (4).
(*b*) Ibid., s. 1 (5).
(*c*) Ibid., s. 1 (6).
(*d*) Ibid., s. 1 (7).
(*e*) Ibid., s. 2 (3), and see Education Act, 1921 (c. 51), s. 128.

Boarders.

As to boarders, it is provided that nothing in Part V of the Education Act, 1921, is to be construed as imposing a duty on a Local Education Authority to receive as boarders in a boarding school provided by them and certified under Part V of the Act :

  (a) children who are resident in a workhouse or in an institution to which they have been sent by a board of guardians from a workhouse or boarded out by such guardians ;(a)

  (b) children who belong to the area of another education authority ;

unless the guardians or the other Local Education Authority as the case may be, are willing to contribute towards the expense of the education and maintenance of such children such sum as may be agreed on between the authorities concerned.(b)

Area to which Child Belongs.

The question to what area a child belongs is to be determined in the manner in which the question to what area a child resident in a charitable institution belongs is determined.(c)   But in the case of a child educated as a boarder in a boarding school so certified the Local Education Authority who are making provision for his education continue liable to make such

(a) See note (a), p. 92, *ante.*
(b) Education (Institution Children) Act, 1923 (c. 38), s. 2 (1).
(c) See p. 92, *ante.*

provision pending the determination of any question which may arise as to the area to which he belongs.(*a*)

It is provided by the Local Government Act, 1929, that for the purpose of determining the area in which the place of settlement of a child is situated under the Education (Institution Children) Act, 1923, the place of settlement shall be deemed to be the parish which would have been the place of settlement if the Local Government Act had not been passed.(*b*)

Higher Education of Blind Children.

On concluding the compulsory period of education at the age of sixteen a blind child may enter on a course of higher education, the object of which is to fit him for some definite vocation. Suggestions for more effective co-operation between the training and employing agencies are made in the Ministry of Health Circular 387 (1923). One of the main diffi- culties in regard to such students, arises from the discrepancy between the wide definition of blindness in the Education Act and that adopted by the Ministry of Health for the purposes of the Blind Persons Act. A student who is blind within the Education Act definition (*c*) may be admitted to a course of training only to find at the end of the course that he is not sufficiently blind to be eligible for employment as a blind person. The Ministry of Health has, accordingly, with the Board of Edu- cation, arranged that no student shall be admitted

---

(*a*) Education (Institution Children) Act, 1923 (c. 38), s. 2 (2).
(*b*) Local Government Act, 1929 (c. 17), Sched. X, r. 18.
(*c*) See p. 63, *ante*.

to such a course unless in the opinion (based on competent medical advice) of the Managers of the Institution and of the Local Education Authority or other contributing body, he either is, or there is a reasonable prospect that by the time his training is ended he will be blind within the Ministry of Health's definition.(a)   If in a particular case it is desired to admit a student who is not likely to become eligible for employment as a blind person, the Managers and Local Authority must satisfy themselves

   (a) that no blind student will be excluded or deprived of training by reason of his admission ;
   (b) that there is a reasonable prospect of the partially blind student being able to earn a satisfactory living in the trade in which he is to be trained without assistance under an approved scheme under the Blind Persons Act, 1920.(b)

Regulations for Higher Education.

The Board of Education recognise courses of instruction primarily intended for students previously educated in Special Schools up to the age of 16.(c) The special conditions applicable to these courses are contained in Chapter 7 of the Board of Education (Special Services) Regulations, 1925, and are as follows :—

   (1) The course must be a full-time course of such

(a) See p. 38.
(b) Ministry of Health Circular No. 681 (1926).
(c) S.R. & O. 1925, No. 835, r. 31.

L. R. B.   H

duration as the Board may require in preparation for a trade and must give progressive instruction in all suitable branches of the trade, instruction in general subjects and appropriate physical training. It must be so conducted as to encourage a corporate life and to afford opportunities for recreation.(a)

(2) The instruction of students must be organised apart from the employment of workers and in separate rooms and under a separate staff, except in so far as the Board may sanction other arrangements.(b)

(3) The course must occupy not less than 40 weeks in each year, and instruction must be given during at least 25 hours per week in not less than 10 meetings held before the hour of 6 p.m.(c)

(4) The Board's approval of a course may be withdrawn if in their opinion a sufficient number of the students do not remain until the end of the course, or if a sufficient number do not on leaving the course enter the occupations for which they have been trained.(d)

(5) The requirements of the Board as to school records and the registration of attendances must be complied with.(e)

(6) No student may, without the permission of the Board, be admitted to a course unless he is prepared to take the whole course, or attend

(a) S.R. & O. 1925, No. 835, r. 32 (1).
(b) *Ibid.*, r. 32 (2).
(c) *Ibid.*, r. 32 (3).
(d) *Ibid* , r. 32 (4).
(e) *Ibid.*, r. 32 (5).

any secular instruction not forming part of a course.(a)

(7) Students who have not previously attended Special Schools may be admitted to the course if they are likely to profit thereby, but no student may be admitted to the course or allowed to continue in attendance who is unfitted so to profit.(b)

The general conditions relating to special services, and set out in dealing with Special Schools, are also applicable.(c)

Grants for Higher Education.

Grants are payable to Local Education Authorities for Higher Education in respect of such of the special services as are services of higher education under Grant Regulations No. 4.(d) The provisions of Chapter 7 of the Special Services Regulations do not preclude the Board from recognising for the purposes of grant under other Grant Regulations expenditure incurred by Local Education Authorities on the higher education of blind students otherwise than by means of the full-time courses mentioned in Chapter 7, but no expenditure will be recognised by the Board of Education under Grant Regulations No. 4 in respect of an institution for the higher education of blind students provided by a Local Education Authority unless the institution complies with the conditions of Chapter 7 of the Regulations

(a) S.R. & O. 1925, No. 835, r. 33 (1).
(b) Ibid., r. 33 (2).
(c) See p. 79, ante.
(d) S.R. & O. 1925, No. 835, r. 1 (3).

or is recognised for grant under some other Regulations of the Board.(a)

Grants are also payable in respect of higher education to institutions not provided by the Local Education Authority. The conditions under which these grants are payable are the same as those under which grants are payable for children in Special Schools not provided by a local authority.(b)

Amount of Grant.

The actual sum payable will comprise :—

(a) a sum in respect of each unit of average attendance, namely £8 10s. for a day pupil, and and £16 10s. for a boarder, and

(b) a sum representing two and a half per cent. of the amount of the salaries paid in respect of employment in the courses to teachers in contributory service, as calculated for the purposes of the Teachers (Superannuation) Act, 1925 (c. 59).(c)

(a) S.R. & O. 1925, No. 835, note to Chapter 7.
(b) See p. 79, ante.
(c) S.R. & O. 1925, No. 835, r. 41 ; S.R. & O. 1931, No. 184, r. 2.

CHAPTER 6.

MISCELLANEOUS PROVISIONS.

THERE are a number of miscellaneous provisions relating to the Blind which it is proposed to deal with in this chapter under their appropriate headings.

AFFIDAVITS.

Where an affidavit is sworn by any person who appears to the officer taking the affidavit to be illiterate or blind, the affidavit must certify in the jurat that the affidavit was read in his presence to the deponent, that the deponent seemed perfectly to understand it, and that the deponent made his signature in the presence of the officer. No such affidavit may be used in evidence in the absence of this certificate, unless the court or a judge is otherwise satisfied that the affidavit was read over to, and appeared to be perfectly understood by, the deponent.

This provision is applicable to proceedings in the High Court,(a) to proceedings in the County Court, (b) and to bankruptcy proceedings.(c) There was formerly a similar provision in the Divorce Rules,

(a) R.S.C. Ord. 38, r. 13.
(b) C.C.R. Ord. 19, r. 10.
(c) Bankruptcy Rules, 1915, r. 15.

but it is now omitted in the Matrimonial Causes
Rules, and a general provision is substituted that
in any matter of practice or procedure not governed
by statute or dealt with in the Rules, the Rules of
the Supreme Court are to apply.(a)

It is essential that the affidavit should be read
over in the presence of the Commissioner. In a case
where the managing clerk of the deponent's solicitor
deposed that he had read over the affidavits to the
deponent before they were sworn, and that the deponent appeared perfectly to understand them, but
it was not deposed that the reading over was in the
presence of the Commissioner, the affidavits were
held to be irregular and were taken off the file.(b)
It has been held otherwise in Ireland where, however,
the Rules of the Supreme Court are not applicable.(c)

Where affidavits had in fact been read over as required, but the jurat stating this had been omitted,
the affidavits were held to be regular and were
ordered to be filed as they stood.(d)

For a form of affidavit, see Stringer's *Oaths*, 4th
Edition, at p. 114, and Daniell's *Forms*, 7th Edition,
at p. 8.

As to affidavit of due execution of the Will of a
blind person, see p. 8, *ante*.

BANKRUPTCY PROCEEDINGS.

See Affidavits, *supra*, and Proxies, *infra*.

(a) Matrimonial Causes Rules, 1924, r. 97.
(b) *Re Longstaffe, Blenkarn* v. *Longstaffe* (1884) 54 L.J. Ch. 516.
(c) *Verner* v. *Cochrane* (1889) 23 L.R. Ir. 422.
(d) *Fernyhough* v. *Naylor* (1875) 23 W.R. 228.

COMPANY WINDING-UP PROCEEDINGS.

See Proxies, *infra*.

DOG LICENCE.

No licence is necessary in the case of a dog kept and used solely by a blind person for his or her guidance.(*a*)

NATIONAL HEALTH INSURANCE.

Blind persons to whom work is given out by or on behalf of any charitable or philanthropic institution, and who are not wholly or mainly dependent for their livelihood on their earnings in respect of that work are not liable to contribute under the National Health Insurance Act, 1924 (c. 38). Their employment as such outworkers is deemed not to be employment within the meaning of the Act.(*b*)

Persons engaged in the part-time service of reading to the Blind are also exempt.(*c*)

POSTAGE RATES.

Special rates of postage are provided for postal packets consisting of books and papers impressed with characters in relief for the use of the Blind. Certain conditions must be complied with. These are :—

(*a*) Customs and Inland Revenue Act, 1878 (c. 15), s. 21.
(*b*) National Health Insurance (Outworkers) Order, 1932, S.R. & O. 1932, No. 307.
(*c*) National Health Insurance (Subsidiary Employments) Order, 1932, S.R. & O. 1932, No. 501.

(a) Every packet must bear on the outside the inscription "Literature for the Blind", and the written or printed name and address of the sender.

(b) Every packet is subject to examination in the post.

(c) Every packet must be posted either without a cover, or in a cover open at both ends and so that the same can be easily removed for the purposes of examination.

(d) No packet may contain any article not being literature for the Blind, except a label which may bear the name and address of the person to whom the packet is to be returned.

(e) No packet may contain any communication or inscription, either in writing or in ordinary type, except the title, date of publication, serial number, names and addresses of printer and publisher, price and table of contents of the book or paper, and any key to, or instructions for, the use of special type.(a)

Subject to the fulfilment of these conditions the postage rates on literature for the Blind are :—

On every packet not exceeding two pounds in weight, one halfpenny.

On every packet exceeding two pounds in weight and not exceeding five pounds, one penny.

On every packet exceeding five pounds and not exceeding six and a half pounds, three halfpence.(b)

(a) Inland Post Warrant, 1923, S.R. & O. 1923, No. 575, reg. 24.

(b) Inland Post Amendment (No. 2) Warrant, 1926, S.R. & O. 1926, No. 1468, reg. 4.

Proxies.

In bankruptcy (a) and winding-up proceedings (b) when a creditor desires to vote by proxy, and such creditor is blind or incapable of writing, his proxy may be accepted if he has attached his signature or mark thereto in the presence of a witness, who must add to his signature his description and residence. All insertions in the proxy must be in the handwriting of the witness, and such witness must certify at the foot of the proxy that all such insertions have been made by him at the request and in the presence of the creditor before he attached his signature or mark.

Travel Facilities.

Certain railway companies and tramway undertakings permit blind persons accompanied by a guide to travel at reduced rates. As these arrangements are made by the companies and undertakings by virtue of their statutory powers in regard to fares and may vary in each case no further details are given here.

Unemployment Insurance.

No contributions in respect of unemployment insurance are payable in respect of persons engaged in the part-time service of reading to the Blind, (c) nor of blind persons who are in receipt of pensions

---

(a) Bankruptcy Rules, 1915, r. 266.
(b) Companies (Winding-up) Rules, 1929, r. 154.
(c) Unemployment Insurance (Excepted Subsidiary Employments and Inclusion) Special Order, 1931, S.R. & O. 1932, No. 43.

under the Old Age Pensions Acts, 1908–1919, as extended by the Blind Persons Act, 1920 (c. 49), section 1.(a)

VOTING.

(1) Bankruptcy and winding-up proceedings, see Proxies, *supra*.

(2) Elections.(b) The presiding officer, on the application of any voter who is incapacitated by blindness or other physical cause from voting in the manner prescribed by the Ballot Act, must, in the presence of the agents of the candidates, cause the vote of such voter to be marked on a ballot paper in the manner directed by such voter, and the ballot paper to be placed in the ballot box. The name and number on the register of voters of every voter whose vote is marked in pursuance of this rule, and the reason why it is so marked, must be entered on a list, in the Ballot Act called " the list of votes marked by the presiding officer ".(c)

The presence of the agents of the candidates refers to the presence of such agents as may be authorised to attend and as have in fact attended, at the time and place where any act or thing is being done, and the non-attendance of any agents at such time and place does not, if such act or thing is otherwise duly

---

(a) Unemployment Insurance Act, 1920 (c. 30), s. 5 (5), as extended by Unemployment Insurance (No. 2) Act, 1924 (c. 30), s. 16, Sched. II.

(b) See the Blind Voters Bill, set out in Appendix III to this work, which was introduced on February 23, 1933.

(c) Ballot Act, 1872 (c. 33), Sched. I, r. 26.

done, in anywise invalidate the act or thing done. (*a*)

(3) **Poll under Sunday Entertainments Act, 1932** (c. 51). The Rules relating to a Poll under this Act contain a provision for the marking of the vote of a voter incapacitated by blindness, in words substantially equivalent to those of the Ballot Act, *supra*.(*b*)

WIRELESS LICENCES.

Blind persons are entitled to free wireless licences by the Wireless Telegraphy (Blind Persons Facilities) Act, 1926 (c. 54). By this Act, where a person satisfies the Postmaster-General that he is a blind person within the meaning of the Act, a licence to establish, maintain and work a wireless telegraph station for the purpose of receiving messages only may be granted to him by the Postmaster-General subject to such terms, conditions, and restrictions as the Postmaster-General may think fit, but without payment of any fee.(*c*)

For the purpose of this Act, a blind person is any person (not being resident in a public or charitable institution or in a school) who produces to the Postmaster-General a certificate issued by or under the authority of the council of the county or of the county borough in which he is ordinarily resident that he is registered as a blind person in the area of the county or county borough.(*d*)

(*a*) *Ibid.*, r. 55.

(*b*) Sunday Cinematograph Entertainments (Polls) Order, 1932, S.R. & O. 1932, No. 828, Sched. II, r. 5.

(*c*) Wireless Telegraphy (Blind Persons Facilities) Act, 1926 (c. 54), s. 1.

(*d*) *Ibid.*, s. 2 (1).

In a Circular of the Ministry of Health it is pointed out that as the council may maintain the register of the Blind either directly or through a voluntary agency, it is for the council to decide whether they will themselves issue the certificate required by this Act, or allow the agency to do so where the agency keeps the register.(a)

The expenses incurred by a council in this matter are to be defrayed in the case of a county council out of the county fund as expenses for general county purposes, and in the case of a county borough out of the borough fund or borough rate. This applies to the City of London as if it were a county borough and the Common Council were the council of a county borough and the general rate were the borough fund or rate.(b)

The licence ceases on the death of the licensee.

(a) Ministry of Health Circular 756 (1926).
(b) Wireless Telegraphy (Blind Persons Facilities) Act, 1926 (c. 54), s. 2 (1).

APPENDIX I.

BLIND PERSONS ACT, 1920.
10 & 11 GEO. 5, C. 49.

An Act to promote the Welfare of Blind Persons.

[16th August 1920.]

BE it enacted by the King's most Excellent Majesty, by and with the advice and consent of the Lords Spiritual and Temporal, and Commons, in this present Parliament assembled, and by the authority of the same, as follows :—

1. Every blind person who has attained the age of fifty shall be entitled to receive and to continue to receive such pension as, under the Old Age Pensions Acts, 1908 to 1919, he would be entitled to receive if he had attained the age of seventy, and the provisions of those Acts (including the provisions as to expenses, but excluding the provisions of subsection (2) of section 10 of the Old Age Pensions Act, 1908, relating to the giving of notices by registrars of births and deaths) shall apply in all respects to such persons as if for the first statutory condition there were substituted a condition that the person must have attained the age of fifty, and be so blind as to be unable to perform any work for which eyesight is essential, and as if for references to " seventy " and

" fifty " there were respectively substituted references to " fifty " and " thirty ".

2.—(1) It shall be the duty of the council of every
county and every county borough, whether in combination with any other council or councils or otherwise, to make arrangements to the satisfaction of the
Minister of Health for promoting the welfare of blind
persons ordinarily resident within their area, and
such council may for this purpose provide and maintain or contribute towards the provision and maintenance of workshops, hostels, homes, or other
places for the reception of blind persons whether
within or without their area and, with the approval
of the Minister of Health, do such other things as may
appear to them desirable for the purpose aforesaid.
The Council shall, within twelve months after the
passing of this Act, prepare and submit to the Minister of Health a scheme for the exercise of their
powers under this section.

(2) The expenses incurred by a council under this
section shall be defrayed in the case of a county
council out of the county fund as expenses for general
county purposes and in the case of a county borough
council out of the borough fund or borough rate.

(3) A council may borrow for the purposes of this
section in the case of a county council in accordance
with the Local Government Act, 1888, and in the
case of a county borough council, in accordance with
the Public Health Acts, 1875 to 1908, but the money
so borrowed by the council of a county borough shall
be borrowed on the security of the borough fund or
borough rate, *and money borrowed for the purposes of*

this section shall not be reckoned as part of the debt of the council for the purposes of any provision limiting the powers of borrowing by the council.(a)

(4) A council may exercise any of the powers conferred by this section (other than the power of raising a rate or of borrowing money) through a committee of the council, and may appoint as members of the committee persons specially qualified by training or experience in matters relating to the Blind who are not members of the council, but not less than two-thirds of the members of every such committee shall consist of members of the council, and a committee established under this section may, subject to any direction of the council, appoint such and so many sub-committees consisting either or partly of members of the committee, as the committee thinks fit.

(5) This section shall apply to the City of London as if it were a county borough and the common council were the council of a county borough, and any expenses of the common council under this section shall be defrayed out of the general rate.

(6) Nothing in this section shall affect the powers and duties of local education authorities under the Elementary Education (Blind and Deaf Children) Act, 1893, or the Education Acts, 1870 to 1919, and local education authorities in the exercise of their duty to contribute to the establishment of a national system of public education available for all persons capable of profiting thereby shall make or

(a) The words in italics were repealed by the Local Government Act, 1929 (c. 17), Sched. XII.

otherwise secure adequate and suitable provision for the technical education of blind persons ordinarily resident in their area who are capable of receiving and being benefited by such education.

(7) For the purposes of this section, a blind person who becomes an inmate of an institution for the blind after the commencement of this Act shall be deemed to continue to be ordinarily resident in the area in which he was ordinarily resident before he became an inmate of such institution.

3.—(1) The War Charities Act, 1916, shall apply to charities for the blind as if it were herein re-enacted and in terms made applicable to such charities, subject, however, to the following modifications :—

(a) The registration authority shall, as respects the City of London, be the common council of the City of London, and elsewhere the county council or county borough council ;

(b) Notwithstanding anything in subsection (3) of section 2 of the Act, the registration authority may refuse to register a charity if they are satisfied that its objects are adequately attained by a charity registered under the Act ;

(c) Notwithstanding anything in section 4 of the Act, the fee payable on registration of a charity may exceed ten shillings, but shall not exceed two guineas ;

(d) Regulations made by the Charity Commissioners under section 4 of the Act shall be subject to the approval of the Minister of Health instead of a Secretary of State ;

(e) Where a charity is removed from the register, the Charity Commissioners may exercise, in relation to the charity, any powers which they are authorised by section 6 of the Act to exercise in relation to charities registered under the Act for the purposes of an appeal thereunder ; and

(f) Where any of the conditions mentioned in section three of the Act are not complied with in respect of any registered charity, any person who, by regulations made under section 4 of the Act, may be made responsible for the observance of those conditions shall be guilty of an offence against the Act.

(2) Regulations may be made by the Charity Commissioners subject to the approval of the Minister of Health for providing that in the case of any charities for the blind which have, before the passing of this Act, been registered under the War Charities Act, 1916, the registration under that Act shall have effect as registration by the appropriate registration authority under this Act and for making such consequential provisions as may be necessary for that purpose.

(3) In this section " charity for the blind " means any fund, institution, or association (whether established before or after the commencement of this Act) having or professing to have for its object or for one of its objects the provision of assistance in any form to blind persons or any other charitable purpose relating to blind persons, but shall not include any

fund, institution, or association where any such object as aforesaid is subsidiary only to the principal purposes of the charity.

4.—(1) This Act shall apply to Scotland subject to the following modifications :—

    (a) Subsections (2) and (3) of section 2 and paragraphs (d) and (e) of subsection (1) of section 3 shall not apply.

    (b) The following subsection shall be substituted for subsection (6) of section 2—

        (6) Education authorities under the Education (Scotland) Act, 1918, shall make or otherwise secure adequate and suitable provision for the technical education of blind persons ordinarily resident in their areas who are capable of receiving and being benefited by such education.

    (c) The expression " county borough " has the meaning assigned thereto in section 132 of the Children Act, 1908, and the provisions of subsection (21) of that section so far as applicable to county and town councils shall apply for the purposes of this Act with the substitution of references to this Act for references to the Children Act, 1908 or any section thereof ;

    (d) References to the Minister of Health and to the Charity Commissioners shall be construed as references to the Scottish Board of Health.

(2) This Act shall apply to Ireland subject to the following modifications :—

(a) References to the Minister of Health shall be construed as references to the Local Government Board for Ireland ;

(b) The expenses incurred by a council under this Act shall be defrayed out of the poor rate, and in the case of a county council shall be raised as a county at large charge, and a council may borrow for the purposes of this Act under Article 22 of the Schedule to the Local Government (Application of Enactments) Order, 1898.

5. This Act may be cited as the Blind Persons Act, 1920, and shall come into operation on the tenth day of September nineteen hundred and twenty.

APPENDIX II.

STATUTORY RULES AND ORDERS, 1920, No. 1696.

THE CHARITIES FOR THE BLIND REGULATIONS, 1920, SEPTEMBER 10, 1920, MADE BY THE CHARITY COMMISSIONERS AND APPROVED BY THE MINISTER OF HEALTH, SEPTEMBER 10, 1920, UNDER SECTION 3 (1) AND (2) OF THE BLIND PERSONS ACT, 1920 (10 & 11 GEO. 5. C. 49).

To the County Council of every County :—
To the Common Council of the City of London :—
To the Council of every County Borough :—
And to all others whom it may concern.

Whereas by section 3 (1) of the Blind Persons Act, 1920, it is enacted that the War Charities Act, 1916, shall apply to Charities for the Blind as if it were therein re-enacted and in terms made applicable to such Charities, subject, however, to the following modifications (*inter alia*) :—

(a) The registration authority shall, as respects the City of London, be the Common Council of the City of London, and elsewhere the County Council or County Borough Council ;

(b) Notwithstanding anything in subsection (3) of section 2 of the Act, the Registration Authority may refuse to register a charity if they are

116

satisfied that its objects are adequately attained by a Charity registered under the Act ;

(c) Notwithstanding anything in section 4 of the Act, the fee payable on registration of a Charity may exceed ten shillings, but shall not exceed two guineas ;

(d) Regulations made by the Charity Commissioners under section 4 of the Act shall be subject to the approval of the Minister of Health instead of a Secretary of State ;

(e) Where any of the conditions mentioned in section 3 of the Act are not complied with in respect of any registered Charity, any person who, by regulations made under section 4 of the Act, may be made responsible for the observance of those conditions shall be guilty of an offence against the Act.

And whereas by section 3 (2) of the said Blind Persons Act, 1920, it is enacted that Regulations may be made by the Charity Commissioners subject to the approval of the Minister of Health for providing that in the case of any Charities for the Blind, which have, before the passing of the said Blind Persons Act, 1920, been registered under the War Charities Act, 1916, the registration under that Act shall have effect as registration by the appropriate registration authority under the said Blind Persons Act, 1920, and for making such consequential provisions as may be necessary for that purpose.

And whereas by section 4 of the War Charities Act, 1916, it is enacted that the Charity Commissioners for

England and Wales may, subject to the approval of the Secretary of State, make regulations—

(a) prescribing the forms of applications under the Act and the particulars to be contained therein;

(b) prescribing the form of the registers to be kept under the Act and the particulars to be entered therein ;

(c) providing for the inspection of registers and lists kept under the Act and the making and the furnishing and certification of copies thereof and extracts therefrom ;

(d) prescribing the fee (not exceeding ten shillings) to be paid on registration, and the fees for making or obtaining copies of, and extracts from, registers and lists ;

(e) requiring notification to the registration authority of any changes requiring alterations in the particulars entered in the register ;

(f) providing for the exemption of charities from the Act and prescribing the grounds of exemption ;

(g) generally for carrying the Act into effect.

Now, therefore, the Charity Commissioners for England and Wales, in exercise of their powers in this behalf and with the approval of the Minister of Health as hereafter signified, do hereby make the following regulations—that is to say :—

1. In these Regulations, unless the contrary intention appears :—

(a) The expression " the Commissioners " means

the Charity Commissioners for England and Wales.

(b) The expression " the Act " means the Blind Persons Act, 1920, and the expression " the 1916 Act " means the War Charities Act, 1916, as re-enacted and modified in and by the Act.

(c) The expression " the Register " means the Register kept by a Registration Authority under the Act.

(d) The expression " Committee " means the Committee or other body responsible for the administration of the Charity.

2. These Regulations may be cited as the Charities for the Blind Regulations, 1920, and shall have effect subject to the provisions of the Act.

3. Every application to the Registration Authority for registration or exemption under the Act shall be made in the forms set forth in the First and Second Schedules respectively to these Regulations and shall be signed by some person or persons duly authorised on behalf of the Charity.

4. The Register shall contain the following particulars with regard to every Registered Charity for the Blind :—

(a) The name of the Charity.
(b) Date of establishment.
(c) The precise objects of the Charity.
(d) The address of the administrative centre of the Charity.
(e) The name and address of the Secretary.

(f) The name and address of the Treasurer.

(g) The full names, addresses, and descriptions of the Chairman and the other members of the Committee.

(h) The name and address of the bank or banks at which the account of the Charity is kept.

(i) The name and address of the Auditor.

(j) The date of application for registration.

(k) The date of registration, and

(l) (if a Charity be removed from the Register) the date of removal.

5. A duplicate of the entries relating to each Registered Charity shall be entered by the Registration Authority on a separate Register Sheet (a supply of which Sheets can be obtained from the Commissioners), and such Sheet shall forthwith be sent to the Commissioners.

6. The Registration Authority shall enter in their Lists of Charities for the Blind refused registration and of Charities for the Blind exempted from registration the following particulars, namely :—

(a) The name of the Charity.

(b) The address of the administrative centre of the Charity.

(c) The precise objects of the Charity.

(d) The name, address, and description of each person applying on behalf of the Charity for registration or exemption.

(e) The considerations which have led the Authority to refuse registration or to exempt the Charity from registration.

(f) The date on which consent of the Minister of Health to exemption was given.

(g) The date of refusal or exemption.

(h) The specified period, if any, for which exemption was granted.

7.   A duplicate of the entries relating to each Charity refused registration or exempted from registration shall be entered by the Registration Authority on a separate List Sheet (a supply of which Sheets can be obtained from the Commissioners) and such Sheet shall forthwith be sent to the Commissioners.

8.   A fee of one guinea shall be paid to the Registration Authority with every application for registration.

9.   Every Account of a Registered Charity for the Blind at a Bank shall be kept in the name of the Charity.

10.   Any changes in the particulars supplied for entry in the Register shall at once be communicated to the Registration Authority, who shall make the necessary alteration in the Register and shall immediately notify the same to the Commissioners.

11.   The Registration Authority shall forthwith notify to the Commissioners the name of any Charity for the Blind which they have removed from the Register, together with full particulars of the reason for such removal and all information in their possession as to the funds and securities of the Charity and the persons holding them.

12.   The Register and Lists shall at all reasonable times be open to the inspection of all persons interested free of charge, and such persons may on pay-

ment of a fee of 3d. make copies of or extracts from
any entry in the Register or Lists relating to a specific
Charity. Copies of or extracts from any such entry
in the Register or Lists shall be supplied to any such
person on payment of a fee of 6d. for each copy or
extract. Such copies or extracts shall be certified by
the signature of the Clerk to the Registration Authority or of some person authorised to act on his behalf
when the copies or extracts are obtained from the
Authority, and by the signature of the Secretary to
the Commissioners or some person authorised on his
behalf if the copies or extracts are obtained from the
Commissioners.

13. Duly audited accounts of every Registered
Charity for the Blind shall be sent to the Registration Authority at least once in every period of twelve
months; but the Registration Authority with the
consent of the Commissioners, or the Commissioners,
may call for such accounts at any time. Such accounts shall relate to receipts and expenditure of
money only : but with a view to meeting the requirements of section 3 (iv) of the 1916 Act, each such
Registered Charity shall keep a sufficient record of all
their dealings with articles in kind of whatever
nature.

14. Any appeal from the refusal of a Registration
Authority to register a Charity for the Blind or from
the decision of a Registration Authority to remove
such a Charity from the Register shall be made to the
Commissioners in writing within 14 days from the
date of the intimation of the refusal or decision or
within such further time as may be allowed by the

Commissioners, and must be accompanied by a statement giving the reasons for the appeal and by any evidence which the appellants may desire to adduce in support of the appeal.

15. The appellants shall at the same time give notice of the appeal to the Registration Authority and the Authority shall forthwith communicate to the Commissioners their reasons for the refusal or decision and the evidence in support thereof.

16.—(1) A Registration Authority may, with the consent of the Minister of Health, exempt from registration under the Act any Charity for the Blind if in the opinion of the Authority the scope of the operations of the Charity as regards the amount of subscriptions expected to be received, the duration of the Charity or the area of collection or of benefit is so limited as to make it unnecessary in the interests of the public that the Charity should be registered under the Act.

(2) In exempting a Charity for the Blind from registration under the Act, the exemption may be limited to such period of time as may be determined by the Registration Authority with the consent of the Minister of Health.

(3) If at any time the Registration Authority should consider that the character of an exempted Charity for the Blind has materially varied in any of the respects mentioned in paragraph (1) of this Regulation, the Registration Authority shall, after obtaining the consent of the Minister of Health, withdraw the exemption.

17. If any bazaar, sale, entertainment, or exhibi-

tion is promoted to raise funds for a registered Charity for the Blind, one of the conditions which the Committee shall impose in giving the approval required by section 1 of the 1916 Act shall be that an account of all receipts and expenditure in connection with the bazaar, sale, entertainment, or exhibition shall be rendered to them.

18. Where any appeal is made to the public for donations or subscriptions in money or in kind to any Charity for the Blind registered under the Act or any attempt is made to raise money for any such Charity by promoting any bazaar, sale, entertainment or exhibition, or by any similar means, the name of the Charity as appearing in the Certificate of Registration shall be stated in full in all posters, bills, circulars, advertisements and notices relating to such appeal or attempt to raise money, with the addition of the words "Registered under the Blind Persons Act, 1920".

19. Every person who is for the time being a member of the Committee of any Registered Charity for the Blind shall be responsible for the observance of the conditions mentioned in section 3 of the 1916 Act in respect of that Charity.

20. Every application to the Commissioners by or on behalf of a Registration Authority or of a Charity to determine the question whether the Charity is a Charity for the Blind within the meaning of the Act shall be made to them in the form set forth in the Third Schedule to these Regulations, shall be signed by some person or persons duly authorised on behalf of the Authority or Charity and shall be accompanied

by full information as to the objects and constitution of the Charity.

21. Where a Charity for the Blind has before the 16th August, 1920, been registered under the War Charities Act, 1916, and on the 10th September, 1920, is still a Charity so registered, the following provisions shall have effect :—

(1) The Committee shall, within two calendar months from the 10th September 1920, or within such further period as the Commissioners may allow, furnish to the Registration Authority under the Act a statement signed by some person or persons duly authorised to sign on behalf of the Committee, containing the same particulars with regard to the Charity, as are required to be furnished under these Regulations by a person applying for the registration of a Charity under the Act.

(2) Where the Registration Authority under the Act, and the Registration Authority under the War Charities Act, 1916, are not the same body, the Committee shall also within a similar period forward to the Registration Authority under the Act a copy certified by the signature of the Clerk to the Registration Authority under the War Charities Act, 1916, or of some person authorised to act on his behalf, of all entries relating to the Charity in the Register kept by that Authority of Charities registered by them under the last-mentioned Act.

(3) The statement received from the Committee

under paragraph (1) of this Regulation shall be compared with the certified copy of the entries in the Register under the War Charities Act, 1916, or where the Registration Authority under the Act is also the Registration Authority under the War Charities Act, 1916, with the entries recorded in their Register under the said Act.

(4) If on the comparison aforesaid it appears that the Charity is the Charity which was registered under the War Charities Act, 1916, the Registration Authority under the Act shall forthwith enter the Charity in the Register of Charities for the Blind, and thereupon the Charity shall be deemed for all purposes to be a Charity registered under the Act as from the 10th September 1920.

(5) Upon the registration of the Charity under paragraph (4) of this Regulation, the Registration Authority under the Act shall send the Charity a certificate of such registration, and no fee in respect of such registration or certificate shall be charged by the Registration Authority.

(6) When the entry of the Charity on the Register under the Act has been completed, the registration under the Act shall take the place of the previous registration under the War Charities Act, 1916, and the Charity shall cease to be a Charity registered or requiring to be registered under the last-mentioned Act.

(7) A note of the registration under the Act, and

of the date and effect of such registration shall be entered by the Registration Authority under the War Charities Act, 1916, on the register sheet relating to the Charity in the Register of Charities registered by them under that Act, and a copy of the entry so made shall be sent to the Commissioners. For the purpose of enabling this entry to be made it shall be the duty of the Registration Authority under the Act, if not the same body as the Registration Authority under the War Charities Act, 1916, immediately upon the completion of the entry of the Charity on the Register under the Act, to transmit the necessary information to the Registration Authority under the War Charities Act, 1916. The latter Authority shall in the like circumstances deliver to the former Authority, if requested to do so by that Authority or by the Committee, any copies of audited accounts of the Charity sent to them in pursuance of section 3 (ii) of the War Charities Act, 1916.

Sealed by Order of the Commissioners this 10th day of September, 1920.

(L.S.)   *G.C. Bower,*
                                    Secretary.

The Official Seal of the Minister of Health has been hereunto affixed in testimony of the Minister's approval of these Regulations.

(L.S.)   *A. V. Symonds,*
                   Secretary, Ministry of Health.

10th September, 1920.

First Schedule.

———

APPLICATION FOR REGISTRATION.

In the Matter of the BLIND PERSONS ACT, 1920.

(1) (We) the undersigned being (a person) (persons) duly authorised on behalf of the
(Insert name of Charity)

Charity
hereby apply to have the said Charity registered under the above-named Act.

The following particulars should be furnished by the Applicants :—

(1) The date of establishment.
(2) The precise objects of the Charity.
(3) The address of the Administrative Centre of the Charity.
(4) The name and address of the Secretary.
(5) The name and address of the Treasurer.
(6) The full names, addresses, and descriptions of the Chairman and the other members of the Committee.
(7) The name and address of the Bank or Banks of the Charity.
(8) The name and address of the Auditor of the Charity accounts.

> *These particulars are required by the Regulations made by the Charity Commissioners under the Act, and it is an offence against the Act to*

make any false statement in an application for registration.

(I) (We) hereby declare that the above particulars are correct in every respect.

Full Name
Signature
Address
Description

Full Name
Signature
Address
Description

Date

Second Schedule.

APPLICATION FOR EXEMPTION.

IN THE MATTER OF THE BLIND PERSONS ACT, 1920.

(I) (We) the undersigned being (a person) (persons) duly authorised on behalf of the
(Insert name of Charity)

Charity hereby apply to have the Charity exempted from the provisions of section 1 of the War Charities Act, 1916, as re-enacted and modified in and by the above-named Act.

The following particulars should be furnished by the Applicants :—

(1) The date of establishment.

L. R. B.   K

(2) The precise objects of the Charity.

(3) The address of the Administrative Centre of the Charity.

(4) The name and address of the Secretary.

(5) The name and address of the Treasurer.

(6) The area within which appeals for subscriptions are confined.

(7) An approximate estimate of the maximum amount expected to be raised by such appeals.

(8) The reasons for claiming that the Charity should be exempted as desired.

These particulars are required by the Regulations made by the Charity Commissioners under the above-named Act, and it is an offence against the Act to make any false statement in an application for exemption.

(I) (We) hereby declare that the above particulars are correct in every respect.

Full Name
Signature
Address
Description

Full Name
Signature
Address
Description

Date

N.B.—By the Regulations made by the Charity Commissioners under the Blind Persons Act, 1920, it is provided that no Charity can be exempted by the Registration Authority from the provisions of section 1 of the War Charities Act, 1916, as re-enacted and modified in and by the said Act, unless the scope of its operations as regards the amount of subscriptions expected to be received, the duration of the Charity or the area of collection or of benefit is so limited as in the opinion of the Registration Authority to make registration unnecessary in the interests of the public. It is further provided that no Charity shall be exempted except with the consent of the Minister of Health.

Third Schedule.

APPLICATION FOR DECISION WHETHER A CHARITY IS A CHARITY FOR THE BLIND.

IN THE MATTER OF THE BLIND PERSONS ACT, 1920.

[I the Clerk to the   Council of   ]

[(I) (We) the undersigned being (a person) (persons) duly authorised on behalf of the Charity   ] hereby apply to the Charity Commissioners for England and Wales to determine the question whether the (Insert name of Charity) Charity is a Charity for the Blind within the meaning of the Act.

The following particulars should be furnished by the Applicants:—

(1) The date of establishment.

(2) The precise objects of the Charity.

(3) The address of the Administrative Centre of the Charity.

(4) The Charity affords assistance to Blind Persons in the manner and to the extent set out below :

These particulars are required by the Regulations made by the Charity Commissioners under the Act.

(I) (We) hereby declare that the above particulars are correct in every respect.

Signature
Address

Signature
Address

Signature
Address

Date

APPENDIX III.

Blind Voters Bill.

MEMORANDUM.

The Bill enables a person incapacitated by blindness from voting alone, to take a relation or a friend to the polling booth to assist him in marking his paper. Under the present law the blind person has to tell the presiding officer in the presence of the local representatives of the candidates for whom he wishes to vote.

There are 58,000 blind electors in the United Kingdom.

A BILL TO

Amend the Ballot Act, 1872, so as to enable any blind voter at a poll regulated by that Act to avail himself of the assistance of a friend, and for purposes connected with the matter aforesaid.

Be it enacted by the King's most Excellent Majesty by and with the advice and consent of the Lords Spiritual and Temporal, and Commons, in this present Parliament assembled, and by the authority of the same, as follows :—

1.—(1) The Ballot Act, 1872, shall have effect as if in the rules for elections set out in Part I of the

First Schedule to that Act, there were inserted after rule 26 the following rule:—

" 26A.—Where any voter who is incapacitated by blindness from voting without assistance, and who is accompanied by another person, makes application to the presiding officer to be allowed to vote with the assistance of the person accompanying him (hereinafter referred to as "the friend"), the presiding officer, if he is satisfied by a declaration made in accordance with this rule that the friend has attained the age of twenty-one years and has not previously assisted more than one person to vote at the election then taking place, shall grant the application, and thereupon anything which is by this Act required to be done to or by the said voter in connection with the giving of his vote, may, notwithstanding anything to the contrary in this Act, be done to, or with the assistance of, the friend, as the case may be.

" The said declaration shall be in the form set out in the Second Schedule to this Act, or as near thereto as circumstances admit, and shall be made by the friend in the presence of the presiding officer and be given to that officer and attested by him.

" The name and number on the register of voters of every voter whose vote is given in accordance with this rule, and the name and address of the person assisting him to vote, shall be entered in a list (in this Act referred to as ' the list of blind voters assisted by other persons ').

" Such a declaration as aforesaid shall be exempt

from stamp duty, and no fee or other payment shall be charged in respect thereof."

(2) Section 4 of the Ballot Act, 1872 (which provides for the punishment of persons infringing the secrecy of the ballot in any manner specified therein) shall have effect as if at the end of the first paragraph of that section there were inserted the words " No person, having undertaken to assist a " blind voter to vote, shall, without the authority " of the blind voter, communicate to any other " person any information as to the candidate for " whom that voter intends his vote to be given or " for whom his vote has been given, or as to the " number on the back of the ballot paper issued at a " polling station for the use of that voter."

(3) The amendments specified in the schedule to this Act, being minor and consequential amendments of the Ballot Act, 1872, shall be made in the provisions of that Act mentioned in the said schedule.

2.—(1) This Act may be cited as the Blind Voters Act, 1933.

(2) References in any Act passed before the commencement of this Act to the Ballot Act, 1872, shall be construed as references to that Act as amended by this Act.

(3) This Act, in so far as it relates to matters in respect of which the Parliament of Northern Ireland has power to make laws, shall not extend to Northern Ireland.

SCHEDULE.

MINOR AND CONSEQUENTIAL AMENDMENTS OF THE BALLOT ACT, 1872.

1. The rules for elections set out in Part I of the First Schedule to the Ballot Act, 1872, shall have effect subject to the following modifications, that is to say :—

  (a) in rule 21 (which requires the presiding officer at a polling station to exclude therefrom all persons except electors, the clerks, the agents of the candidates and the constables on duty) there shall be inserted after the word " candidates " the words " any person accompanying " a blind voter for the purpose of assisting him " to vote " ;

  (b) in paragraph (5) of rule 29 (which specifies the things which a presiding officer must seal up and deliver to the returning officer on the conclusion of the poll), after the words " tendered votes list " there shall be inserted the words " the list of blind voters assisted by other persons", and after the words "unable to read " there shall be inserted the words " the declarations made by persons assisting blind voters to vote " ;

  (c) in rule 38 (which requires certain documents relating to an election to be forwarded by the returning officer to the Clerk of the Crown in Chancery), after the words "tendered votes list", there shall be inserted the words " lists of blind voters assisted by other persons ", and after the words " statements relating thereto ", there shall be inserted the words " declarations made by persons assisting blind voters to vote ".

2. The Second Schedule to the Ballot Act, 1872, shall have effect as if the following form were inserted therein :—

Form of declaration to be made by a person assisting a blind voter to vote.

" I, of , hereby declare that I have attained the age of twenty-one years, and that I have not previously assisted any person [except of]a to vote at the election now taking place.

(*Signature of the person making the Declaration*)........................

(*Date*) ....

" I, the undersigned, being the presiding officer for the polling station for the [county]a [borough]a of , hereby certify that the above declaration, having been first read to the above-named , was signed by him in my presence.

(*Signature*) ....

(*Date*)............ : (*hour*).........

" N.B.—If the person making the above declaration knowingly and wilfully makes therein a statement false in a material particular, he will be guilty of an offence."

(*a*) Strike out the words in square brackets, if inappropriate.

APPENDIX IV.

WELFARE OF THE BLIND.

*Regulations made by the Ministry of Health,
7th August, 1919.*

(These Regulations ceased to have effect after March 31st, 1930, but they are still of importance as a guide to Local Authorities.)

Voluntary Agencies.

Circular 7.
B.D.
MINISTRY OF HEALTH,
WHITEHALL, S.W. 1.
7th August, 1919.

SIR,

I am directed by the Minister of Health to state that an estimate has been laid before Parliament for a grant to be distributed in aid of certain services carried on for the benefit of the Blind.

This grant, if voted by Parliament, will be appropriated in aid of these services for the period from 1st July, 1919, to 31st March, 1920. Thereafter, subject to the consent of Parliament, a grant will be payable in respect of each financial year ending on the 31st March.

The grant will be available in respect of the follow-ing services :—

(1) Workshops for the Blind.
(2) Provision of assistance to Home-Workers.
(3) Homes and Hostels for the Blind.
(4) Home-Teaching.
(5) Book-Production.
(6) The work of Counties Associations.
(7) Miscellaneous.

Regulations governing the distribution of the grant are appended.

The Minister is very conscious of the needs of the Blind generally, and of the large amount of valuable work done on behalf of the Blind by the voluntary agencies interested in their welfare. He is aware also of the many difficulties, financial and other, en-countered by these agencies in carrying out their work as they would wish. Amongst the larger problems in this field of work is that of arriving at satisfactory arrangements for relieving the lot of the unemployable blind living in their own homes. For this there is no pecuniary provision in these Regula-tions, for the reason that none such is possible until suitable legislation has been passed ; this is not at present practicable, but a promise has been given that proposals will be laid before Parliament as soon as possible. These Regulations, therefore, are, from the larger point of view, a temporary expedient, yet one which it seems clear should not be held back, pending the passing of fresh legislation ; for it is confidently believed by the Minister, in concurrence with the opinion held by the Advisory Committee on the Blind, that, pending legislation, the system of grants now to be introduced will materially assist in improving the conditions of the Blind in many directions.

The Regulations have been drawn up with as much elasticity as is consistent with the efficiency of the services for which grants will be payable, and it will be observed that room is left for local initiative in the formulation of schemes. I am 'particularly to draw attention to the provisions of paragraph 20 of the Regulations with reference to the formulation of schemes in connection with Home-Workers, and in this connection I am to say that while the Minister is of opinion that, wherever practicable, employment in a workshop is preferable to provision of assistance to workers in their own homes, it is recognised that, in a number of cases, home-work may be necessary. For the guidance of agencies which desire to submit schemes it is suggested that the needs to be met may include :—

(a) Supply and maintenance of full complement of tools and equipment which are necessary for executing work satisfactorily.

(b) Supply of materials at lowest market prices, including delivery.

(c) Assistance in making and finishing articles and inspection of articles.

(d) Advice as to current prices.

(e) Marketing the finished article, including advertising.

(f) Arrangements for periodic returns as to output·

I am to explain that the object of paragraph 14 of the Regulations is that any conditions which are unhealthy or unsatisfactory may be reviewed, as for example, in a workshop where regard would be had to the number of workplaces which can properly be provided in view of the extent, arrangements and sanitary conditions of the workshop and the nature of the trades practised.

As regards approval of agencies generally, the Minister will require to be satisfied not only of the efficiency of the arrangements made for carrying out the services, but also of the necessity for providing the services in the particular area. He will not be prepared to approve any agency which is conducted for private profit in any way.

With regard to Home Teaching the Minister desires to make the following observations. At present it is apparent that there is a pronounced shortage of Home Teachers, and he would be glad to see this service so far extended as to admit of one teacher being employed for every 50 blind persons taught in an urban area and for every 30 in a rural area. This service appears to offer scope for the employment at an adequate salary of the better educated blind person whose qualifications are otherwise suitable, and the Minister trusts that the grant will encourage the extension of Home-Teaching throughout the country.

It will be observed that under paragraph 33 of the Regulations the Minister is prepared to consider applications for grant in respect of miscellaneous work carried on for the benefit of the Blind, and he would particularly welcome any considered scheme for research work in new industries for the Blind or for work in connection with the prevention of blindness. He would be prepared also to consider schemes for assistance to skilled workers in occupations other than those usually practised in workshops.

The Minister would be glad, in the interests of the Blind themselves, to see more co-operation between the several agencies, more particularly in regard to workshops, and it will be observed that one of the general conditions of grant is that the services to be aided must be co-ordinated between separate agencies so far as is practicable. The Minister trusts that every effort will be made to secure such co-operation.

I am to draw your attention to the rules for keeping registers, which are scheduled to the Regulations. The registers should be commenced not later than the 1st September, 1919, and all agencies concerned will be expected to furnish the Ministry with such records in respect of the months of July and August as may reasonably be required. Model registers are being drawn up and copies will be obtainable in due course from His Majesty's Stationery Office through the usual channels.

The Regulations contemplate the observance by every workshop of the recognised standards of the trade in which its employees are engaged so far as they affect rates of pay, bonus, hours of labour, and holidays. If any question arises as to the compliance or non-compliance by any workshop with these standards, the point at issue will be referred by the Minister to the Minister of Labour for determination.

The Minister trusts that an equitable and effective administration of these Regulations will be greatly facilitated by the services of the Special Inspectors recently appointed to the Staff of the Ministry, who have had many years of practical experience in all branches of work for the Blind.

It should be noted that the Regulations may be altered at any time by the Minister in such manner as may seem desirable or may be rendered necessary by the passing of legislation dealing with the Blind, but due notice will be given to all agencies concerned of any proposed alterations.

   I am, Sir,
    Your obedient Servant,

      ROBERT L. MORANT,
The Secretary.   *Secretary.*

Regulations under which Grants will be paid by the Minister of Health in aid of the Welfare of the Blind.

1. In these Regulations the expression " the Minister " means the Minister of Health, and the expression " agency " means an institution, society or body engaged in work for the Blind.

2. Grant will be payable to approved agencies in respect of the following services :—

(1) Workshops for the Blind.
(2) Provision of assistance to Home-Workers.
(3) Homes and Hostels for the Blind.
(4) Home-Teaching.
(5) Book-Production.

(6) Counties Associations.

(7) Miscellaneous.

3. An agency will not be approved by the Minister except after consultation with the Council of the appropriate County or County Borough and unless :

(a) its arrangements for carrying out any of the services mentioned in Article 2 of these Regulations are satisfactorily co-ordinated so far as is practicable with similar arrangements made by other agencies, and are of such a nature as to afford assistance to a suitable number of blind persons ;

(b) the agency is not conducted, either as a whole or in respect of any service, for private profit ;

(c) the conditions laid down in Part I of these Regulations are, so far as they may be applicable, observed by the agency.

PART I.

General Conditions of Grant.

4. (a) Grants will first be payable to an approved agency under these Regulations in respect of work done during the nine months commencing 1st July, 1919. Thereafter grants will be paid for financial years commencing 1st April.

(b) During the period or year there will be paid an instalment of the grant for that period or year. The instalment may be at a rate not exceeding fifty per cent. of the estimated grant for the period or year.

(c) The balance of the grant will be paid after the

end of the period or year when the audited Statement
of Accounts and any other return required by the
Minister have been received from the agency.

(d) The Minister may, at his discretion, reduce or
withhold a grant. In any decision as to payment
of grant, regard will be had to the standard of efficiency of the work in respect of which a grant is
claimed.

5. The premises and work of the agency shall be
subject to inspection at all reasonable times by any
of the Minister's officers.

6. The agency shall keep accurately and in the
manner directed by the Minister such records and
registers, and shall supply to the Minister such returns
or other information as he may, from time to time
require, and all such records and registers shall,
when so required, be available for inspection by the
Minister or his officers. The rules contained in the
Schedule to these Regulations shall be observed by
the agency in keeping the Registers to which they
relate.

7. The accounts of the agency shall be audited
annually by a member of the Institute of Chartered
Accountants, or of the Society of Incorporated
Accountants and Auditors, or by a Banker or Bank
Manager, or, with the special consent of the Minister,
by some other person not being the Secretary or
Treasurer of the agency. All accounts shall be kept
in such manner as the Minister may from time to
time direct, and shall be made up to the 31st March
in each year, unless the Minister otherwise directs.

8. The agency shall be under the management of a

L. R. B.   L

properly constituted Committee of Management with duly appointed officers, including a Secretary and Treasurer.

9. Any application for grant shall be made on a form to be supplied by the Minister.

10. Any person in respect of whom grant is claimed shall be a person who is blind within the definition adopted by the Minister, that is to say, too blind to perform work for which eyesight is essential.

11. Due security shall be given, in such manner as the Minister may approve, that the services or any of them carried on by the agency shall not cease without 12 months' notice having been given to the Minister, and that, if the Committee of Management, Owners, Managers or Trustees are unable or unwilling to carry on the services or any of them until the expiration of the period of notice, they shall refund to the Minister such proportion of any instalment of a grant as is properly represented by the unexpired portion of the period in respect of which grant has been paid.

The amount of grant payable in respect of any service which ceases to be carried on by the agency shall not, in any case, exceed the liabilities of the agency in respect of that service.

12. If, in any case, the instalment of a grant paid in respect of any service is larger than the total amount of grant finally payable, the agency shall refund to the Minister the difference between that amount and the amount of the instalment.

13. A grant will not be payable in aid of any service in respect of which grants are payable by the

Board of Education or other Government Department.

14. For the purpose of assessing the amount of grant to be paid the Minister may exclude any item and may deduct any proportion of the amount claimed, which, in his judgment, represents an excess over the total amount properly payable having regard to the conditions under which the service is carried on.

15. If any question arises as to the interpretation of these Regulations the decision of the Minister shall be final.

PART II.

Rates of Grant and Special Conditions in respect of the Several Services.

Workshops.

16. The expression " workshop employee " means a blind person who is regularly employed by an approved agency in or about a workshop for the Blind, and in receipt of weekly pay at the Trade Union or other standard rate customary in the particular class of work on which the blind person is employed, and who is not a pupil undergoing training or an apprentice.

The expression " working day " means that portion of any day on which the workshop is open, the expression " meeting " means either of the customary morning or afternoon portions of a working day, and the expression "attendance" means, in respect of a meeting, attendance for the whole of the meeting.

17. Grant will be payable to the agency at a rate not exceeding £20 per head per annum in respect of the total number of workshop employees in regular employment throughout any period, that number being computed as the quotient of the total number of attendances during the period divided by the number of meetings during the period.

18. The recognised standards of the trade in which the workshop employees are engaged so far as they relate to rates of pay, bonus, hours of labour and holidays must be observed by the agency. In no case may the hours of labour exceed 48 hours per week.

Provision of Assistance to Home-Workers.

19. The expression "home-workers" means adult blind persons who, for sufficient reasons, are employed elsewhere than in a workshop in occupations usually practised in workshops and are attached for the purposes of care, assistance and supervision to an approved agency.

The expression "tools and equipment" means the actual instruments necessary in the occupation followed by a home-worker, and does not include material or clothing.

20. The agency shall submit to the Minister, in the first instance, a scheme whereby suitable provision is made for the care, assistance and supervision of

home-workers, and the Minister may before accepting any scheme require such modifications to be made in it as he thinks fit. The scheme shall include arrangements for the maintenance of the necessary tools and equipment, the supply of materials to the workers, the supervision of, and assistance in, the making of the article, and the marketing of the finished article, and shall be accompanied by full particulars of the numbers and sex of the home-workers for whom provision is proposed to be made, the nature of the occupations practised, and details of the method to be followed in carrying out the scheme, including details as to the prices to be charged for materials supplied to the home-workers and as to prices to be paid for finished articles purchased from the home-workers.

21. Grant will be payable at a rate not exceeding £20 per annum in respect of each home-worker included in a scheme accepted by the Minister and regularly employed throughout any period.

22. A grant will be payable in aid of the initial expenditure incurred by the agency in the provision of the tools and equipment necessary to enable a home-worker included in a scheme accepted by the Minister to follow his occupation.

The grant will normally be half of the expenditure incurred after the consent of the Minister to the expenditure has been obtained.

23. The agency shall supply to the Minister such reports upon the working of an accepted scheme as he may from time to time require.

Homes and Hostels.

24. The expression " Home " means a residential institution for the care and maintenance of adult blind persons who, owing to age or infirmity, are incapable of work, and are in need of accommodation which cannot be provided otherwise than in an institution.

The expression " Hostel " means a residential institution for the provision of board and lodging for blind workers.

The expression " maintenance days " means, in relation to any blind person resident in a Home or Hostel, the number of days from midnight to midnight during which the blind person is maintained in the Home or Hostel, the day of admission and the day of leaving being counted as one day.

25. Grant shall be payable to a Home at a rate not exceeding £13 per annum and to a Hostel at a rate not exceeding £5 per annum in respect of each of the blind persons regularly resident throughout any period in the Home or Hostel, the number of such persons being the quotient of the total number of maintenance days divided by the number of days in the period for which grant is claimed.

26. A blind person towards whose maintenance in a Home a contribution is on the 1st of July, 1919, being paid by any Board of Guardians shall not be reckoned as a resident for grant purposes under these Regulations unless the rate of contribution then being paid in respect of such person is maintained, nor shall any person admitted to a Home at a future

date by agreement with a Board of Guardians be reckoned as a resident for grant purposes under these Regulations unless the rate of contribution is not less than half of the average rate of cost per head of maintenance in the Home.

For the purpose of this paragraph the cost of maintenance in a Home shall include all the expenses incurred in or about the maintenance and care of the residents in the Home.

Home-Teachers.

27. For the purposes of these Regulations, the expression " Home-Teacher " means a person paid and employed by an approved agency to teach adult blind persons in their own homes how to read embossed type, to read to them, and to instruct them in simple forms of home occupations.

28. Grant will be payable at a rate not exceeding £78 per annum in respect of each Home-Teacher employed by an agency with the consent of the Minister, provided that such consent will not be required in respect of a Home-Teacher employed by the agency prior to the 1st July, 1919, and continuing in the employment of the agency after that date.

Book-Production.

29. Grant at the rate of 2s. 6d. per volume, and at the rate of 2d. per copy of a magazine, periodical or sheet music will be payable in respect of all literature produced in embossed type for the Blind by an approved agency.

Counties Associations of Agencies.

30. The expression "Counties Association" means the Association of agencies operating in any group of Counties for which a Local Advisory Committee has been constituted, and the expression "Counties Association area" means the Counties in any such group. A Counties Association shall be deemed to be an agency for the purposes of paragraph 3 of these Regulations.

31. Grant will be payable to a Counties Association at a rate not exceeding £20 for every 100 blind persons resident in the Counties Association area and registered on the 30th September in any year in the central register kept at the Ministry of Health.

32. It shall be the duty of any Counties Association, being an approved agency, to submit a scheme to the Minister for rendering financial assistance out of any grant received to the agencies affiliated to the Association, regard being had not only to the general work carried on by such agencies, but to the necessity for securing the registration of all blind persons.

Miscellaneous.

33. The Minister will be prepared to consider an application from an agency for a grant towards the expenditure incurred or estimated to be incurred in any service, other than the services mentioned in these Regulations, which has for its object the betterment of the conditions of the Blind or the prevention of blindness.

SCHEDULE.

Rules for the Keeping of Registers.

A.

General Rules.

1. The name of the agency must be distinctly written on the cover of each register ; and on the title page there must be the signature of the Secretary, Manager, or Superintendent, and the date on which the register was commenced.

2. The pages of all registers must be numbered consecutively, no leaf may be inserted in or withdrawn from any register, and no blank space left between the entries.

3. Entries must be original and not copies, and must be made in ink without erasure or insertion.

If it is necessary to make any correction, this should be done in such a manner that the original entry and the alteration made are both clear on the face of the record.

During any time in which registers are at the Ministry of Health for inspection, under paragraph 6 of the Regulations, the necessary records must be kept in a temporary register, and the totals be transferred to the original registers as soon as these are returned. The temporary register must be preserved.

B.

Special Rules.

1. *Workshops.*

4. Every workshop must have :—

    (a) a register of admission ;
    (b) an attendance register ;
    (c) a register of summaries.

4. (a) Admission Register.—An entry should be made in the admission register for each workshop employee on the first day he attends the workshop. The name of an employee should be removed as soon as he ceases to attend the workshop and it is ascertained that he is unlikely to resume attendance.

This register must show for each employee :—

(1) the date of his admission ;
(2) his name in full and address ;
(3) if he has left, the date of his last attendance.

4. (b) Attendance Register.—This register must show the name of every workshop employee entered on the admission register.

There must be a column for the attendance or absence of every employee to be entered at each meeting, and each of these columns must be properly dated before any entry of attendance or absence is made in it. The columns must be grouped in months and at the foot of each there should be spaces for entering the total number of employees present and the total number withdrawn before completing an attendance (Regulation 16).

The attendance register must show clearly on the cover the customary hours of opening and closing the workshop in respect of each meeting, and the register must be closed within 20 minutes of the customary hours of opening.

Every employee whose name has been entered in, and has not been removed from the admission register, must be marked ⌣ (present) or O (absent).

The mark of presence of any employee who leaves before the customary hour of closing must be cancelled at once by drawing a ring round it thus ⊘. The number of employees whose marks of attendance have been cancelled must be entered each day in the space provided.

4. (c) Register of Summaries.—At the close of each month or part of the month during which the workshop has been open, the following entries must be made in the register of summaries in respect of that period :—

(1) The number of working days.
(2) The number of meetings.
(3) The total attendances.
(4) The average attendance.

2. *Homes and Hostels.*

5. Every Home and Hostel must have :—

(a) a register of admission ;
(b) a register of maintenance days ;
(c) a register of summaries.

5. (a) Admission Register.—An entry should be made in the admission register for each resident on the first day of admission. The name of a resident should be removed as soon as he leaves the home or hostel otherwise than with the intention of resuming residence.

This register must show for each resident :—

(1) The date of his admission ;
(2) his name in full and address : and, if he ceases to be a resident ;
(3) the date of leaving.

5. (b) Register of Maintenance Days.—This register should show the name of every resident entered in the admission register.

There must be a column for each day in which the presence or absence of every resident must be entered and each of these columns must be properly dated before any entry of presence or absence is made in it. The columns must be grouped in months, and at the foot of each there should be spaces for entering the total number of presences and the total number of absences during the month.

The appropriate column of the register of maintenance days must be entered up daily.

Every resident whose name has been entered in, and has not been removed from the admission register, must be marked ⌐ (present) or O (absent). A resident shall be deemed to be absent if he is continuously away from the Home or Hostel for a period of 18 hours, and shall be deemed to be absent in respect of every subsequent continuous period of

24 hours during which he remains away from the Home or Hostel.

Provided always that residence in a branch home may be reckoned as residence in the Home.

5. (c) Register of Summaries.—At the end of each month during which the Home or Hostel has been open, the following entries must be made in the register of summaries in respect of that period :—

(1) The numer of days.
(2) The total number of residents marked present.
(3) The average number of residents marked present.

INDEX.

A.

AFFIDAVIT,

 blind person, of, bankruptcy proceedings, 101
     County Court proceedings, 101
     divorce proceedings, 101, 102
     form, 102
     High Court proceedings, 101
     reading over, 101
 due execution of Will of blind person, of, 8

ASSISTANCE,

 meaning of, alternative to poor relief, as, 57

B.

BANKRUPTCY,

 proceedings, affidavit of blind person, 101
    proxy of blind person, 105

BEQUEST,

 blind, for, charitable, whether, 10, 11
 charitable, construction of, 12-14
      amalgamation of charities, 13
      branch, gift to, 13
      change of name, 13
      misdescription of charity, 12
   validity of, 12

BLIND,

 definition, Education Act, 63
   Ministry of Health, of, 38
       test applied, 39
  pension, for, 60

[1]

INDEX.

INDEX.

INDEX.

C.

CERTIFICATE,

agency, by, evidence of blindness, as, 61

employment as workshop employee, of, evidence of blindness, as, 61

exemption from registration, blind charity, of, 32

medical, boarding-out, in case of, 70

              suitability for Special School, of, 78, 79

registration, blind charity, of, 24

              blind person, as, wireless licence, for, 107

school for the Blind, as, conditions for, 61

              of, evidence of blindness, as, 61

CERTIFIED SCHOOL,

grant to, amount of, 91

              calculation of, 90, 91

local authority, boarding-out by, near, 67

              contribution by, to, 67

              maintenance by, of, 66, 67

regulations. *See* SPECIAL SCHOOL.

report to Parliament by Board of Education, 85

requirements, 75

CHARITY,

definition, 10

              exemption from income tax, for, 16, 17

trade carried on by, exemption from income tax, 17

CHARITABLE INSTITUTION,

meaning of, education of children out of own area, 93, 94

CHARITY COMMISSIONERS,

appeal to, refusal to register charity for the blind, on, 25

combined register of, 29

consent of, prosecution under Blind Persons Act, 36

decision of, administrative centre of charity, as to, 19

              charity for the Blind, particular charity, whether,

                                      21

INDEX.

INDEX.

INDEX.

[7]

Index.

INDEX.

HOSTEL,
> inmates of, registration of, 47
> provision of, local authority, by, 48

I.

INCOME TAX,
> exemption from, charity for the Blind, 14
> > charity of, Schedule A., 15
> > > Schedule B., 15
> > > Schedule C., 16
> > > Schedule D., 16

INFANTILE OPHTHALMIA,
> definition, 55
> notification, 55

INSTITUTION,
> non-provided, grant to, amount of, 91
> > calculation of, 90, 91
> subscription to, local authority, by, 58
> unemployable Blind in, powers of local authority as to, 57, 58

INSURANCE,
> National Health, blind outworker, for, 103
> unemployment, pensioned blind person, 61, 105

L.

LEGACY,
> *See* BEQUEST.

LIBEL,
> publication of, blind person, to, 4

LICENCE,
> dog, blind person, for, 103
> wireless, blind person, for, 107
> > expenses of, 108

INDEX.

M.

MINISTRY OF HEALTH,
>approval of, regulations under, Blind Persons Act, 18
>consent of, exemption from registration of blind charity, 31,
>>32
>>exemption from registration of blind charity,
>>withdrawal of, 32
>>exercise of powers of local authority as to poor
>>blind children, 58
>>subscription to institution by local authority, 58
>definition of blind, 39
>responsibility for welfare of the Blind, 38
>schemes for welfare of the Blind, powers as to, 48, 49
>schemes of, grants for services for the Blind, 40, 41

N.

NATIONAL HEALTH INSURANCE,
>blind outworker, for, 103
>reader to blind person, for, 103

NEGLIGENCE,
>blind person, injury to, by, 5
>contributory, blind person, by, 5
>local authority, of, children, towards, supervision, as to, 64, 65
>>provision of conveyance
>>without attendant, 64
>railway company, of, 6
>signing document, in, 3

O.

OPHTHALMIA NEONATORUM,
>definition, 55
>notification, 55

OUTWORKER,
>blind, National Health Insurance, 103

INDEX.

P.

PARENT,
    guardians of union, whether, 89
    who is, 89

PAUPER,
    blind, 56–60

PENSION,
    blind person, for, 60, 61
            age, 60
            degree of blindness, 60
            residence in United Kingdom, 60

POOR RELIEF,
    assistance under Blind Persons Act instead of, 56, 57

POSTAGE RATES,
    literature for the Blind, on, 103, 104

PROXY,
    blind creditor, of, 105

R.

RAILWAY COMPANY,
    responsibility to blind passenger, 6

REGISTRATION,
    Blind, of the, 47
            difficulties in case of children, 51
            form of, 50
            responsibility for, 50
    charity for the Blind, of. *See* CHARITY FOR THE BLIND.

RELIGIOUS EDUCATION,
    blind child, of, boarded out, when, 70, 87
            school other than public elementary, in, 86
            public elementary school, in, 86

REMOVAL,
    blind poor person, of, 59

INDEX.

S.

[12]

INDEX.

[13]

INDEX.

W.